For Lisa: A Glimpse into forced adoption, and Robot Middle class Professionals. A Secret World You Won't See

By Thomas Jones Bsc, LLB (Law)[1] 7 August 2020

Contents

Introduction to "For Lisa:" *2*

The Case "for Lisa" *34*

Lisa's Life Story *47*

Detailed Adoption Law *54*

Threshold of Harm in Child Adoption *57*

Human Rights *66*

Important Statistics 75

Duty to Return Child/ Fix Problems *86*

Lisa's Right to Have Say *90*

The Social Workers *98*

Foster Care Cover-Ups 104

---

[1] Details about this author: Thomas Jones Bsc, LLB. Thomas Jones (or Jones, T. (2020) Bsc, LLB holds a Bachelor of Science (Bsc) which includes 50% content in the 'social sciences:' psychology and sociology. Thomas Jones also holds a law degree (LLB).

Adoption Contact Research *110*
Adoption Must Be Last Resort *123*
Conclusion *131*

Introduction to *"For Lisa"*

This paper although more like a book is for a little girl who I refer to as Lisa and her family. For the academic and professional readers, I provide lots of sources throughout including relevant family court statistics. For Lisa is in two parts: a general discussion this introduction of the terrible situation burdening young public law families in the first part, and the detailed Case for Lisa with various statistics within also detailed research in the second part.

This book For Lisa is for all those families and children who suffer in the secret world that people do not see which is forced: *adoption*, *foster care*, *special guardianship*, and being deprived of the right to a family life or the family court version: *Contact*. This paper concerns a mother who was trying her best to challenge an adoption order the judge had made against her daughter, Lisa. Lisa, only about 4 or 5 years of age at the time was removed from her mum and dad to live with middle class strangers in a forcible adoption. Lisa was put in a final adoption placement for the reason that her mum was a domestic abuse victim. Lisa is just one child of the many who are forcibly put in foster care, placement for adoption, or special guardianships. I so name the paper after her, 'For Lisa.' I never got to meet Lisa to know anything about her or her family. I just knew of her case facts and that was forced adoption which as a decent person I felt had a moral responsibility to try to do something about the situation. I wrote the case below for Lisa to give her a chance and the content is true.

Lisa is also just one child of the many parents who have to suffer in silence. It is for these children and families I dedicated this book as well as my own family who believe in me and other people on social media who I have come to know as friends, some of whom have encouraged me to publish For Lisa. Of the families I help I mostly only get to see their plight through words on social media platform so-called "Face book." I need to put away ideas of playing with words and just tell the reader how it really is as I see it based on my experiences. I will be here as candid or frank as humanly possible. In the world I have come across which I think is may be 3 years ago now I began helping families in what is known as secret world or a world of forcible child adoptions. Others in the campaign against child adoptions use the terms 'forced adoption.' The family court professionals use 'non consensual adoption' which means the child is adopted without parental consent. Other family members are not considered in the issues of consent. Face book for me in the family court situation has just become about many, many faces representing the tens of thousands of families who suffer injustice in this secret world of forced adoption. It is a virtual world that is Face book where in the secret world of forcible adoption becomes reality in a world supposedly free or democratic practising United Kingdom that people outside do not see. Since then and every day to this day I have regularly seen the same faces which are often of the domestic abuse young mothers who also often show pictures of their young children. These children are lost to this frightening forcible adoption system or what I see as a child trade if I am still being frank. I receive a private message 'PM' on Face book or someone else will link ('tag') me to someone else on there, who needs my particular type of help or support. A picture of the person who does the PM-ing is usually shown on the message. When I look at these young faces realising they are often so young, I expect them to be out and about with friends, shopping, just generally having fun and enjoying life in a free country as young mothers should. That regrettably is not the reality I have to come to know. I see faces one day and some faces of the young mothers I never see again. I do not know if the young mothers have commited suicide because they have lost children to forced adoption, have been put in prison for trying to contact adopters, have been sectioned under the mental health law because they cannot cope with the loss of a child, or in hospital for physical problems but coming about through the mental strain of a child being forcibly removed. When I say forcible adoption, I also mean foster care and special guardianship as these are all related public law matters because they all have what I will call forcible cross over in the world of forcible adoption. For me it is all related orders including the barely 16 hours a year contact for foster families. The many faces in the family court situation on Face book makes me think of the words or lyrics from certain musicians' bands past and in a relatively recent present. It makes me think of the popular band 2 Unlimited for the Face book families' situation for their involvement with the secret family courts. 2 Unlimited are or were a dance music band around in the 1990s. It was one of their songs that strike a chord with me. As I look back to that time I remember 2 Unlimited words "*faces, all around I see faces….some are happy, some are in misery.*' On Face book I see more misery than happiness. I see faces representing mental anguish and suffering. On that note also the late 60s to early 70s rock band The Doors has the lyrics *"people seem strange when you're a stranger."* I suppose it is easy to take away children when the families to you are just a stranger. It is harder to care for a stranger even if that stranger is just a domestic abuse victim a victim of her circumstance. The family court professionals in my experience helping these families in the secret world of forcible adoption are clearly detached from the stranger families who are already seen as "problem families."

The social worker or for the local authority to be able to remove Lisa has to produce a statement called a social worker's template, which is supposed to consider genuinely Lisa's best interests. The Child's Guardian or CAFCASS Guardian also writes a detailed statement for Lisa's Best Interest. In reality the local authority best interest for the child where adoption has been chosen is always painting the adoption route as perfect and the best route. It is looked at as "adoption for life" and considers

Lisa's life from the angle of the adopters raising Lisa 'for life.' There are never any best interests that I am aware of through all the family court bundles I have been able to see which look at the situation where children such as Lisa were to stay with the domestic abuse victim mother. Most of the time I am shown scanned images from the parents' android phone which are taken of the child's or children's family court bundle. The scanned image shows extracts of the family court statements but with personal details such as child names and address scribbled out of fear that the judge or other family court professionals involved find out that they have been speaking to others about these matters. They are frightened of telling anyone what is going on in the family courts because everything is secret and they are gagged. I talk about this secrecy or what it means to be gagged in part 1 below. I therefore for those reasons decided to put in writing the merits or good things about Lisa's case which I seen as needing to talk about the situation of Lisa and her mother's situation from the other way around. What I mean by that in For Lisa I take a look at what Lisa's best interests would be from the view as though I could see what was going on in this little child's and mother's lives whose wishes and feelings have been ignored by the family court professionals in the family court. I for instance provide a section called Lisa's Life Story which is a little biography as though Lisa stays with her domestic abuse victim mother. As the true situation from the families' point of view is never put in writing in these ridiculously long bundles which can be up to 4000 pages, or even more actually. I felt it necessary to put the true and best interests for Lisa and that would be what this young child and her mother would have genuinely wanted were she to have returned to her mother. The family court judges or non qualified 3 panel magistrates who make adoption orders would normally never get to see this ideal version. The judges who make the adoptions only get to see the versions from the family court professionals. There is a lawyer for the families or each of the parties whether this is mother or father. The lawyer however is connected to local authorities because of the problems and limits with legal aid. I talk about the legal aid situation under the professionals in this part below.

I go in to some detail with the law of adoption in part 2 to show the reader just what parents are up against in terms of the complexities of the adoption law alone. I did my best to help Lisa and her family using my education and apparently my lateral or unique ways of seeing things. Despite my best efforts for example providing Lisa's mother with statements to court, a final adoption was eventually made. Although no consolation for Lisa or her mother, I did manage to write a statement to successfully postpone the final adoption hearing having explained the options available to the family court to give the family a fighting chance. Those details are not included for this paper For Lisa. Neither are the paper work guides I made for the mother as I have done for several other families in related situations or little ideas I use to help the families. Everything is true in the Case For Lisa at part 2 below as

I said above except for the necessary name and location details.

There is support for such families as Lisa and her domestic abuse victim mother on a positive note, often through other parents who have experience of the system, one of whom helped write statements to the family court judge on behalf of Lisa's mother. Regrettably for all the work I/ we put in it was not enough. It was never going to enough; for all my hard work helping families moreover it is never enough in the family courts. It is because the family courts have already made a decision to adopt and nothing under the heavens will stop that sadly. Even though the family was represented in court by a family friend who either knew law or was a middle class professional for instance it was not enough for the family court. Lisa was adopted.

Lisa for that matter was forcefully adopted against her clear wishes (see below) because her mother was a domestic violence relationship as above. Although looking at the law with my legal hat on it should require passing a relatively high degree of harm to remove a child for foster care or adoption. I talk about the law of the threshold which is also the law of significant harm required to remove children. Parliament which makes children law for example use the words **significant** *harm*. Regrettably the law in the United Kingdom and all European Union countries actually, allows children to be removed where the mothers are domestic abuse victims. On that note, I also provide various academic sources for domestic abuse including from lawyers and experts in the USA below. The UK family courts often uses the words '*future emotional harm*' because this now apparently qualifies as significant harm, for even against young mother victims of domestic abuse those who I help daily. The reality is senior social workers and psychologists and psychiatrists associated with the child protection system start campaigns to Parliament to make emotional harm a reason to remove children. It is the gospel according to the middle class, is my opinion. One such campaign was by the children's charity NSPCC campaigning to ban smacking children in the UK. I talk about the NSPCC in my other paper: Introduction to Tyranny as there is a conflict of interest with family court orders. Future emotional harm is often used by the social workers when there is little else to go on. It is like a plan B or plan C contingency. What is interesting is countries outside the EU territories do not use future emotional harm to remove children. One such country is Northern Cyprus that said the rest of Cyprus falls within the EU. I next explain the family court situation generally.

Besides Lisa and her family in forced adoption, it is important to explain what I have learned generally. The information below is intended to show the reader what goes on the secretive family courts. For this purpose I use the formal family court case structure for challenging an adoption. The structure for instance has the form of the typical court case template with names of the parties. I do this because it provides at least a glimpse into the secret world of forced adoption for what goes on in terms of its formalities and rigour in the family courts behind its walls.

I use my academic work as a bit like art to express my self although it is expression through words not pictures. In For Lisa and in my other papers these are an extension of that written expression. The law of adoption is also known as public law. Generally public law means any type of public authority such as police, local authority or the family courts. I started my research into public law practice in the area family courts around the time I was completing my law degree with honours around 2017. Around this time I use to help online through a website I came across called Legal Beagles, a place offering support for various legal problems. Since then I have been helping the families in the world of forced adoption etc. As well as helping these families who I recently began referring to 'public law families,' I have along the way found it necessary to research relevant professional publications for a broad understanding of the situation. I make such comments from my research findings throughout this paper.

It is mainly the public law families who are affected by the so-called 'secret' courts incidentally. My paper is about public law although there are families in the private law situation: family versus other family members. I use the term *public law families* because they are affected by public law in the family courts, for example, foster care, adoption, special guardianship through what is known as the public law outline (PLO). The PLO means the routes such as adoption. Public law in the family court situation means here social services remove children through the Children law. I also frequently in other papers have used the terms *I-phone: families/ parents/ generation* simply because most of the families I come across only have access to an android phone to defeat their family court enemies. There is no computer, scanner or often no social capital to defeat what I quickly come to identify as a well organised army of family court professionals. For me I see it is as a fight through organised family court professionals against the public law families where these robots possess what the sociologist Bourdieu calls *social capital*: university educated and years of family court practise which produces concise although detailed professionally family court bundles for example. It is a war against social class moreover. I help these families for free and what I do can also be considered what lawyers would say is *pro bono* ('for the public good'). I have been doing this pro bono stuff online with the families for at least a couple of years.

For context purposes I use the fictitious family names in For Lisa not necessarily to protect the families' identity. It is never about the need to protect the child and families as if though that made matters worse for the public to find out. That is not the real reason for secrecy regardless of the beating drums sounding out from the family court for the "child's best interest." It is more about protecting

the families from threats of prison or loss of child contact
– not that contact is even a genuine option for many of
these public law families in the secret world of forced
adoption. I want to here in this part 1 also explain what I
mean by secrecy to give the reader if just a glimpse into
the world of forced adoption. The families are not
allowed to talk outside of court about these things
because the judge has made an order not to do so which
often has terms such as contempt and punishment could
include 'prison' and reduced contact with the child. This
is the degrading treatment for the families who personally
experience it daily, and I who am privileged to see it
through court paper work, in these secret courts or what it
means to be "gagged." Think of gagging as having
something like a thick cloth inserted into and filling the
mouth with no ability to talk except making mumbling
noises which cannot be understood. This is life in the
family courts for what happens every day to the public
law families. For balance I discuss the former president
of the family court judge, president Munby who makes it
clear that the family courts should not be secret or

gagging families by saying "*the public needs to know and be confronted with what it is going on.*"

Besides the nightmare of the speed through which adoptions take place all within 6 months. The truth is after adoption contact is rarely a consideration for the family court professionals mainly for reasons I go into below. For those reasons in this paper I provide examples of public law based what should happen with the families in public law matters but in practice in my experience working with these families does not. In For Lisa I intend this work to provide a critique on family court professionals, the judges et cetera, from the view of the affected families. I have to because no one else is or will be so blatant. I next talk about some procedure before Lisa's case in the law of adoption.

In the family courts to remove children such as Lisa it requires following the rules: Family Procedure Rules (2010) and Civil Procedure Rules (1998). FPR and

CPR are actually law used in the family courts. In reality these are baby law compared to Parliament Acts. There are also specific court forms for a child removal. The social workers are allowed to put on the relevant court form adoption from the beginning. For balance below I discuss Featherstone (2018) paper on social workers roles in forced adoption from the association of social workers. It becomes clear that social workers are incredibly under pressure and there is an adoption train that cannot be derailed even when the social worker wants to stop the decision for an adoption. Each social worker will have an average of 17-40 family case loads (see below). The reality is the money train has started to roll to its destination and that cannot be derailed.

It is not just about the law or what the professionals have already decided that little Lisa and her domestic abuse mother have to confront. It comes down to money to pay for legal representation. There is typically no legal aid to pay for lawyers once the judge has made a placement for adoption order. In For Lisa the stage of this paper surrounds the last chance to challenge the adoption of Lisa. This is called oppose the final adoption. It means there was no legal aid to pay for a decent barrister to argue her case.

Lawyers in the family court refer to 'overriding' interest when something more important has precedence. There is also an overriding objective which should mean the parties are treated fairly: "equal footing" regardless of whether one is the powerful local authority and the other is poor young domestic violence victim dependent on legal aid. Families in practice however, do not normally get legal aid to pay for a decent or in fact any solicitor or barrister once a placement for care or placement for adoption order is made. The case needs to be considered very good before that happens. The care order is followed by the placement for adoption order or Plan B: special guardianship in the same final hearing. Family court practice is shockingly bad; the local authorities provide the solicitors and barristers with employment. This is about business and the family court lawyers are no exception. The reality is legal aid requires many cases to make it worthwhile for the law firms. Commercial law as an example, it is possible for the firms in London to make around 3 million or more a year. Solicitors in family law require many public law families on legal aid to make it worth their while. The solicitors will also be over-burdened with case loads. One parent told me when in court their solicitor kept disappearing; it transpires he was seen in other court rooms representing other "clients" at the same time. In the police station the same things go in there with Police Station Representatives paid by legal aid, which means they have taken over the roles of duty solicitors. The parent is literally left in limbo hoping someone online, may be another parent who has their own experience of the broken or corrupt public law system to help them navigate the family court system. This is the elephant in the family court room no one wants to talk about.

As for challenging adoptions in the family court these are as rare as hens' teeth. The first option to stop an adoption is after the judge makes the care order and placement order for the local authority to find suitable adopters. This is called a revoke by the parents of the adoption under *section 24, Adoption of Children Act 2002*. The exception is if the child is placed with the adopters the parents can no longer revoke. Social workers often place the child with adopters and often do not tell the parents. It means the parents have been denied their legal right to revoke the adoption. There is now a foster to adoption where the care order plus the adoption placement order is made at the same hearing. I have seen one judgement for the foster to adoption for a large family around 70 pages long as this included an injunction to stop the family reporting the case to anyone. As is the case in this paper For Lisa, an adoption can also be ***opposed*** under the law of adoption when the adopters decide that they want to adopt the child such as Lisa. I believe it is after 10 weeks of the child living with the adopters that the adopters can apply to adopt the child permanently. The Case For Lisa at part 2 is the stage where adopters have made an application to court in also what is called a final adoption.

The main option besides to revoke and oppose the adoption is to try and appeal the court orders within 21 days. There are extensions to the 21 days in some circumstances. The thing is the parents are told by their lawyers they cannot appeal the care/ adoption/ foster to adoption because they have no grounds to appeal. They are blatantly lied to. The truth is it will mean the lawyers who are provided with work will have to go against the local authorities which provide them regular work. It is also 'jobs for the boys' in that if an appeal is taken by a good or decent independent solicitor or barrister for parents there will be a chance of an appeal; if not there is probably no chance whatsoever. It requires what they see as 'prospects of success.' However, if the parent brings to appeal for adoption for foster care decision their self, there is likely no chance. The Weber speed, timing, without regard for the person has meant the appeals have been streamlined to stop appeals in the family courts. There is a law known as *section 54 (4)*, *Access to Justice Act 1999* which means the judge has the power to refuses appeals just on the appeal statement alone. This law has likely been used more often by appeal judges to refuse appeals than the average family court professional or lawyer's keyboard which letters have since faded.

A family court judge even up to a High Court, or probably, a Court of Appeal, is just an ex solicitor or barrister with about a few years on the job experience. This may sound reasonable so I provide the training required to be lawyers and a judge in a bit for a sobering balance. Before I do that I will explain the appeal situation. One thing about the appeal system is that appeals in the family court are heard by judges below high court. The appeal courts normally are high court, court of appeal and UK Supreme Court. The family courts have a separate appeal system where appeals are appointed to slightly senior judges known as 'circuit judges' although below high court level. The problem you have is the same circuit judges who hear appeals are often the same judges who give adoption orders in other families' cases. Circuit judges are likely grammar school educated and typically white males in their 60s or older. My point is these are incredibly out of touch. Now the families who come before them are can be as young as 17 and domestic abuse victims. One appeal I tried to help was a 3 panel magistrates and the appeal court circuit judge refused the appeal even though the social workers illegally rushed through the adoption to place child with gay men. The system is just sick and more about the power elite, obsessed with power, title and prestige as the sociologist Max Weber predicted.

There is no legal requirement for a lawyer to have a law degree in the United Kingdom. It just requires a 2.1 degree in any subject. I now have to pause at that and still shocked to this day. A 2.1 means second class degree at university equivalent to a B grade. So it is quite high as it second highest to the first class degree grade. In the best universities in the country for instance Oxford University and Cambridge and others exams are heavily used for assessment. To balance this, the best or elite universities are more like examination factories so it is not that hard to get the high marks for the degrees where it is almost normal. For all the normal universities performance in exams is not so great. A little game is played. The main marks at university are weighted as times 1 for second year and times 2 for third and final year. Third year is harder than second year so the game is the normal universities have exams at first year which are not included in the 2.1 grade also in the second year which means the university degree grade is not as how it appears. Even the universities that do law degrees play this game. Academia is such an illusion. It means the apparently high grade law degree is more like an average 2.2 or C grade or lower if it is based on like for like.

My law tutor was Oxford University educated and never did a law degree. At the time I never really thought about it. In the family court situation it is fair to say that law is not in the lawyers' blood I now realise. With only 5-10 years a solicitor or barrister can become a family court judge. A solicitor or barrister can become a slightly senior which is called a circuit judge. The title is 'His Honour' or 'Her Honour.' To become a solicitor it is just a two year training contract plus an expensive one year legal practice course *plus* a three year law degree; or any degree with a one year law conversion course. For a UK barrister it requires the same qualifications as the solicitor although instead of the training contract there is a one year barrister's legal practice course: two sixes or 2 six month periods. They may boast 2.1 or higher normal degrees but it is a bit like driving around in a mini car with the manufacturers badge for a luxury car such as an Aston Martin or Rolls Royce. Many universities do law degrees online. The system is just about money as a legal practice course for a solicitor costs between £16000 and £20,000. Each year in a normal university costs £9,000 per year. You do the math. This is a type of the sociologists' Ritzer's McDonaldisation and Max Weber's modern view of rules at the least. For instance speed, efficiency, and timing without any real quality. At worse the public law families are represented by lawyers with high degree grades but more like something you can get for free out of Kellogg's Cornflake boxes. Now you know why you believe you are more intelligent that the lawyer representing you. They may use big words in long sentences but so would you if you were if you were those middle class persons.

There is now a route for a Legal Executive to become a qualified lawyer requiring no law degree also, just a diluted progression through soft academic and practice modules. I looked at the exam paper and answers for the legal executive at level 6 which is supposed to be equivalent to the final year of the law degree. Soft academically is putting it lightly.   In the USA, for balance to become a lawyer it requires a 4 year degree plus a juris doctorate (US version of the English law degree) in addition to passing the bar exam.   The solicitors' offices now have legal executives that delegates work to paralegals or putting it another way delegating to the unqualified lawyers. Is the UK Weber or Ritzer's McLawyers perhaps? The situation is extremely dire legally speaking for the public law families.

The alternative is to pay for a McKenzie Friend, a sort of 'learn as you go' pseudo lawyer, often a parent who has gone through the courts and learnt the rules and then charges another family for services rendered.   Is this sounding like the sociologist Max Weber's Air of Capitalism?' One McKenzie Friend ('MKF') boasted he has had sexual relations with a family court solicitor. The problem with McKenzie Friends, whilst some may be good there is no legal thinker at work to help the families. There are the more expensive professional MKFs for instance a retired medical Dr, former police officer for instance. Former police officers also become police station representatives although spending years on the other side it is bit like a social workers becoming a lawyer. I cannot see that working except a diluted lawyer. Practically, and commercially, the courts allow McKenzie Friends (lay helpers) as it is keeps the economy going and better that, in the court's view, than be consumed with 'difficult parents' who cannot organise their case. In short, McKenzie Friends make the job easier for the ex solicitor/ ex barrister family court judge.

The courts for the Weber treatment operate a 26 week window limitation as supposed guide for adoption judges. In reality this 26 week is often practice. I show what really happens in the case below. The family court professionals are essentially running around like headless chickens, investigating and producing reports at break-neck speed despite the fact each one of them has an overriding duty to the court to be fair, impartial, and objective. In civil procedure, ie the more expensive suing cases each lawyer hires an expert witness and each is cross examined and what remains is 'the final evidence.' This does not happen in family courts. The public law families get grilled like the Spanish Inquisition for sometimes two days. The middle class foster carers or special guardians are barely examined, maybe for 30 minutes. It is the same for the court appointed experts. Many times these experts are not called for cross examination because "they're busy." The barristers are the qualified family court advocates. These earn up to 300,000 a year. Public law families are lucky if their solicitor (if they have rights as advocates) cross examines the family court professionals never mind having a barrister.

On the family court experts I have seen documents where they have used third and fourth hand hearsay accounts and the professional usually a psychologist (regulated) will produce a statement based on that. The information comes from a visit by the experts to the foster carers or special guardians. In one case of a forcible adoption not only did the appointed psychologist copy and paste paragraphs out of a social worker expert's book on emotional harm they also used a minimum wage earning member of staff via email or telephone for evidence of significant harm which to my horror the court accepted. I know about the social worker's book because I copied and pasted the same paragraphs from that psychologist report and found the book. This psychologist was also the consultant psychologist to a mother and baby unit where the mother's child was forcibly adopted based on that evidence. This proves the psychologist just did not care one iota as it is all about the money. These psychologists can earn anything from up to a million or more a year. One earned at least 400 million as they were registered as a limited company at Companies House. The comical thing is the expert opinion according to that baby law I said above is it must be "necessary." The family courts are more creative and necessary becomes possibly to keep that money train rolling as it knows family court reform will never come.

Ironically although it seems predictable, my research shows these family court professionals have been highly scrutinised as below. The problem is the courts are secret and use the rhetoric 'hide the identity of the child.' Nothing ever gets out. It's a game really, a game of 'find the threshold (significant harm) if the threshold document needs some more sentences to make it look more attractive to a judge so be it. It is done.

There are proponents for open courts but of course these professionals (who the system benefits) want to be there. I think this is bit like a Nazi recording a Nazi murder during the holocaust and showing other Nazis. For the professionals, see my critique on professionals under the 'risk society' below. The legal professionals have a Transparency Project which is biased as they cannot very well 'bite the hand that feeds you.' These are part of the child protection system and transparency means attacking parents cases which have been aired but never attack the professionals who benefit from the world of forced adoption. I note persons who question the professionals in the transparency project pages are patronised or any complaints about social workers, call them 'rare'…recounting their subjective lawyers careers in public law. Alas with necessary digressing above, I now present the case I wrote for 'For Lisa.'

The Case "For Lisa"

The following is 'The Case "For Lisa,"' which is a glimpse into what I identified later as a family court tyranny. This second part is the law of adoption that destroyed a non middle class family and forced little Lisa to live with middle class strangers for life, all because as I said above her mother was a domestic abuse victim. I have removed the normal requirement of numbered paragraphs in For Lisa. This is England in 2020; I have to keep reminding my self that and the fact I am suppose to live in a democratic or free country as when I read law I believed that to be the case. I now know in the family courts there is neither freedom nor democracy.

Case No: X (scheduled hearing date: 5.8.2018)

IN THE FAMILY COURT AT LONDON;

AND IN THE MATTER OF AN APPLICATION
UNDER SECTION 47,
ADOPTION OF CHILDREN ACT 2002;

AND IN THE MATTER OF:
LISA: D.O.B 05/08/2013

BETWEEN:

JANE SPENCER

Applicant

AND –

PAUL GREEN

1st Respondent parent

AND –

THE CHILD ('LISA')
(Through the child's CAFFCASS Guardian)

2nd Respondent

AND -

THE COUNCIL OF THE CITY OF LONDON

3rd Respondent

Miss Jane Spencer representation for opposing the
adoption of Lisa: section 47, Adoption of Children Act
2002 (hereafter 'ACA 2002')

I, Ms Jane Spencer[2] (hereafter 'Ms/ Miss Spencer (also
see my human rights)[3] or 'the parent'; the child's mother;

---

[2] Miss Spencer reminds the judge of the court's overriding duty of
the White Book 'Equal Footing' and commensurate case law. Miss
Spencer informs London Family court that she is LIP; the local
authority barrister is an 'officer of the court, so must answer or
clarify a point of law with regards to adoption law based on the
content of this representation. This young woman does not have

or this woman' et al), of 127 Carlton Street, Brixton, London L56 3YH make this statement knowing its

---

access to her court bundle so DX access encryption services should be considered for her.   Miss Spencer is a fictitious name and is provided for context only.   The same applies to the fictitious child names 'Lisa,' London family court, London local authority, and other family names mentioned elsewhere.

[3] Jones T. (2019) applies the human rights and qualification to a woman in her early 30s whose young child was taken just based on a few raised voices. The local authority viewed it as 'domestic abuse:' (also see op cit Clemente P.) Miss Spencer reminds London family court of her human rights which cannot be interrupted by the inferior family courts (lower than High Court, at the least., as these Convention Article rights ordinarily go beyond all frontiers, save 1) a '*legitimate aim*' and 2) a '*principle of proportionality.*' The term *qualified right* means said public authorities cannot interrupt the family's ('original family members') human rights except *"by law*," only where "….*necessary in a democratic society, in the interests of…public safety, for the prevention of disorder or crime"* (ie **qualified right**).

In any event the measure said public authorities take against Miss Spencer and her family must be *proportionate* and *sufficiently serious*: R (Daly) [2001, HL].[3] On the same human rights' theme, '*necessary in a democracy*' has been defined by the UK Privy Counsel first [1998] UKPC 30,[3] and afterwards by the Court of Appeal [1999] 1 AC, as requiring: **i)** *justification for any limits on fundamental rights*; **ii)** *rationally connected*; **iii)** *no more than absolutely necessary*: De Freitas.

contents to be true, acknowledging its use as evidence for the purposes of London Family Court which I intend to support opposing the adoption of Lisa with the adopters.[4]

Miss Jane Spencer representation for opposing the adoption of the child, Lisa: Leave (Permission)

Miss Spencer seeks the benefit of your honour's discretion under *Adoption of Children Act 2002 ('ACA 2002'), section 47* to oppose[5] my child Lisa's adoption. It is the mother's understanding the barrier to oppose is at the reasonable parent standard. The reasonable parent means just the average parents who is not perfect and is

---

[5] The rules for understanding law are the following. Parliament in London makes the law and the judges' responsibility is to follow what Parliament has said in the law. Parliament Act ie Adoption of Children Act is the main law in the law of adoption.. A Parliament Act is also called a statute. The judges' role in the legal system is to interpret or make sense of the adoption law. The judges' role is called statutory interpretation.

not necessarily compared to an educated or middle class parent. It just means a normal mother from a normal background even where the local authority is classed a deprived one (see below). This young woman moreover wishes to exercise her legal right to a genuine remedy to oppose Lisa's adoption.

Permission to Oppose

Ms Spencer understands that she first requires leave to oppose the adoption of Lisa. Permission here means the same as leave. Permission is required because when the judge has made a placement for adoption tragically for the Spencer family this meant that Ms Spencer whilst still the biological parent of mother was no longer the biological mother based on law. The same applies to Ms Spencer maternal or extended family in addition to Lisa's father and his paternal family. Here leave to oppose Lisa's adoption is so requested to your honour.

In addition to permission to oppose, the London Family Court adoption judge must understand that Child adoption (or what it is in effect) is forced child adoption. Forced adoption is a serious human rights[6] abuse in a modern country with freedoms.

Forced adoption[7] moreover is not only barbaric, as the Court of Appeal judge President Munby pointed out it is such as drastic step that it must be no other option as it will affect Miss Spencer and all of her family for the rest of their lives. According to the Council of Europe, also below the United Kingdom has the harshest type of child adoption in all European countries, which is similar to Canada and the United States of America which are also strict.

Lisa also has a sense of her birth/ family identity insisting that she is 'Lisa Spencer.' This can be verified in the

---

court bundle at contact: ''goodbye' contact. See paragraph titled 'ascertainable wishes/ feelings' (see below).

Miss Spencer in the alternative will either appeal the entire placement for adoption order, or ask for a judicial review.[8]

Ms Spencer will here speak candidly about her view of Lisa's adoption which for an average parent as this mother in a free country has the right to do so. Lisa's adoption for Ms Spencer was either illegal or unlawful as per paragraphs below because Miss Spencer was informed that Lisa would be taken by the local authority under a 'section 20' agreement[9] in that Lisa would only be held 'temporary.' Temporary shall be defined in its

---

[9] Section 20 makes it easier to take child without the need for a court order at the beginning. Social workers force parents to sign or threaten to call the police. The police would be there if they were needed.

ordinary day use. Miss Spencer's Lisa was never returned as a matter of fact; on the contrary, Lisa, a very young blonde blue-eye child (hence *commercially attractive for 'adoption matches'*) was not put in care but immediately transferred to 'foster to adoption' placement.

Miss Jane Spencer representation for opposing the adoption of Lisa: *after Adoption Contact: section 51A, ACA 2002*

Post adoption Contact[10]

Miss Spencer besides permission to oppose the adoption of Lisa also seeks 'face to face' Contact[11] with Lisa in the

---

[10] The law in the United Kingdom is in place for direct contact ('open adoption') between the adopted child and the birth family through the *Children and Families Act 2014*. It rarely if ever happens (see below).

interim period for herself and for the Spencer family. It understood that this mother requires permission for post adoption contact as set out in this paragraph and here makes this request. Ms Spencer in particular relies on the words *"or an order under section 26 [or 51A] (contact): s.1, (7), ACA 2002).*

Miss Jane Spencer representation for opposing the adoption of Lisa: Change of Circumstance

Besides permission to oppose the adoption, it is Miss Spencer understanding that to oppose that there is a further requirement. She for example must show a change of **change of circumstance**:[12] *s.47, ACA 2002.*

---

[11] As far as I am aware there was never any mention of after adoption contact for the mother or her daughter, not even for child relatives of Lisa which stands in the face of her human rights and Child Convention Rights. I talk about Lisa's rights in detail below.

The *change of circumstances* is also at the reasonable parent standard which is set out above. Ms Spencer says there have been material (significant) changes in circumstances. These will be explained here. I will firstly briefly explain the situation as to how social services became involved which led to Lisa's removal from Ms Spencer care.

Previous domestic abuse problems alleged DV perpetrator too near

In short, Miss Spencer was in a domestic abuse relationship, also allegedly viewed by the local authority to be a risk as she was allegedly living too close to the DV perpetrator. Removing Lisa when Miss Spencer was

---

[12] Note the family court at opposing adoption level never consider whether the court was right to make the care order/ placement for adoption/ foster to adoption in the previous judgement where they are all made at the same time. The court's view if the judgment was wrong the remedy is to appal. It is a joke shop as they know hardly any of the public law families win at appeal. This is just the illusion of appeal even if granted a hearing which I call auto cue reading what it is already on the sheet.

at her most vulnerable state[13] (in her mind and behaviour) meant simply it further victimised an already victimised Miss Spencer, which could happen to any one even family court professionals and judges (Birchall, J. et al).[14]

This young woman now has the benefit of a rather luxurious home suitable for herself and Lisa to benefit from for life (see Munby below for a discussion on adoption being the very last resort). Her uncle has made this available as Lisa and her mother have been invited to

---

[13] Miss Spencer likely did not have sui juris (capacity) as she signed section 20 as victim of domestic abuse (vulnerable) and in any event, did so through what Miss Spencer understood to be temporary – that is to say Lisa would be given back to Miss Spencer. Had Miss Spencer known the implications she simply would not have signed (ultra vires therefore).

[14] Recent research into the relationship with family court and women victims suffering domestic violence ('DV') reveals that 68% of DV was raised in court proceedings: Birchall, J., Professor Choudhry, S., and Pallet, P., N.(2018). What about My Right Not To Be Abused, Domestic Abuse, Human Rights and the Family Courts, Women's Aid & Queen Mary University of London School of Law. https://1q7dqy2unor827bqjls0c4rn-wpengine.netdna-ssl.com/wp-content/uploads/2018/05/Domestic-abuse-human-rights-and-the-family-courts-report.pdf

live in her uncle's big house in Scotland and to live there for as long as Ms Spencer has need.[15]

Law is one thing but human realities are entirely different when a child is literally forced away from the only mother she knew since being born to her, which some academic writers equate to 'silent violence,' (Moor, M. Phd (2005)[16], because except criminal assaults there is likely no assault or trespass on a child than the violence of the forceful removal of a child. It is simply a terrible indictment of justice in a democracy that this happens where her mother was a victim of domestic abuse only. I now provide for the court looking at Lisa's situation which is a novel way of looking at things than normally with the family court or the local authority or other

---

[15] Public law families may have richer middle class relatives but don't want to necessarily leave their own communities where they have grown up close to family or have friends. They may not even get on with the middle class relatives. The mother had to move to Scotland but I don't think the mother was happy being away from her family and friends etc. It didn't make a difference anyway as the judge still made the adoption final.

[16] Moor, M. Phd (2005), Australia's Stolen White Children.'

family court professionals such as the voice of the child through Cafcass Guardian. I next introduce Lisa's Life Story.

Miss Jane Spencer representation for opposing the adoption of Lisa: *Lisa's life story: 'Born Lisa Spencer.'*

Lisa's life story

Lisa was born 9 June 2013 to Miss Jane Spencer and Mr Paul Green. Lisa was named 'Lisa Green' (taking the surname of her biological father Paul Green) on her birth certificate. Lisa has had from her 9 June 2013 birth date to have a relationship with her mother Ms Spencer – that is a relationship which necessary in a democracy. By this I mean necessary in a free country where there are assumed to be such rights.

Lisa, prior to her removal was established in life that is to say she was settled insofar as she was attending mainstream education systems, had a mother and father, forged friendships with her peers and was loved by her family. Her family since there has been a placement for adoption are now under the law of adoption known as *'original family members.'* The local authority plans supported by the child guardian is 'adoption for life.' Ms Spencer here will present a different more positive situation for Lisa. Instead of being adopted, Lisa would likely have had a good life in London, be loved and respected by her family, may have went to university and or worked hard at school to make a good life for her self in her other chosen career destinations. When of age, she would have likely met or married a local gentleman of similar age and had her own children to love and care for just as her (not middle class) mother loves her and had done the best for her. In short, there is no reason to believe that Lisa would not have had a good life in London.

Subsequently, Lisa has had 5 years from her birth date to live with and be cared for by her mother – that is also necessary in democracy. Lisa was raised in London, Lisa's home city, and prior to her removal (for reasons she doesn't really understand), forced to live with stranger grownups 'for life,' expected to like other stranger's children.' It is no coincidence that this particular London local authority is considered relatively in poverty when compared with other local authorities in the United Kingdom. Had Lisa and her family benefitted from a section 17 post lottery (see APPG below), her mum and dad would likely have got support from the local authority to deal with the so-called domestic abuse to help them the family stay together. In any event, Lisa will likely miss her mother, Ms Spencer incredibly in a way in which the London local authority or the London family courts will never understand. This version will never be known to Ms Spencer if the adoption is finalised except contact by yearly letter which is almost automatic than any genuine attempt to keep the public families in contact with what will be the adopted child or children.

Lisa is a child with feelings and forcing her to live with complete strangers on a psychological level could simply be devastating for this little child in both the short term and the longer term.

Miss Jane Spencer representation for opposing the adoption of Lisa: *Miss Spencer background*

Article 8 ECHR, and Section 20 [17]

---

[17] A *section 20, Children Act 1989* is usually a voluntary agreement the parents sign to have the child put in care. It is actually a backdoor that local authorities try to use to avoid court but many parents nowadays are more savvy. M.J. Allen, B. Thompson, (2011), p.94 discusses public law broadly which provides a good understanding for the local authority's power or limitations to take action: "the Executive or any civil authority or government official cannot exercise a power unless such exercise of it is authorized by some specific rule of law:" Allen cites Lord Camden CJ in Entick v Carrington (1765) 19 St Tr 1030, in Chapter 3 Rule of Law: Section 2: Government According to the Law, Cases and Materials in

Miss Spencer signed a section 20 agreement at some point prior to her 27 February 2018 'final goodbye contact' with Lisa. Miss Spencer's daughter Lisa was removed just through allegations of domestic abuse in that the London local authority claim there is a risk of future emotional harm to Lisa; as raised voices apparently meet the threshold in the liberal state.[18] Miss Spencer's and Lisa's child Article 8 human rights and child convention rights were automatically engaged at the point the local authority threatened to move Lisa from Miss Spencer care or alternatively the point when the local authority moved Lisa from Ms Spencer care (Munby in Re B-S). It meant that the local authority was

---

[18] It is interesting that social workers view the liberal state in terms of being soft with parents but lawyers and Jones T. view liberal state as being so draconian to remove children from parents who may argue in front of the child occasionally (only requires one incident by law). See Lord Wilson for when the threshold has not been crossed, below.

required to pass the human rights tests notwithstanding a qualifying interest (as above).

Ms Spencer is a litigant in person (no lawyer) who shockingly does not have access to her court bundle by DX (electronic bundle) so is not able to do key search or navigate her court bundle efficiently, contrary to the family court professionals who do and can. For instance, Miss Spencer without an electronic court bundle is not able to challenge the local authority or Cafcass key arguments which support forced adoption by copy and pasting from the bundle documents. Her solicitor apparently told her she does not have legal grounds to challenge forced adoption, a rather complex law as it entails European child law and domestic law (*ACA 2002*). She was for instance informed she had no grounds to oppose or appeal the adoption of her daughter Lisa.

Ms Jane Spencer representation for opposing the adoption of Lisa: *Child adoption law: s.1 (2), (4), (7) (adoption decision/ contact), ACA 2002*

Since Ms Spencer is asking for the judge's discretion to oppose the adoption of Lisa, she reminds him that as the adoption judge he must apply the full adoption law for her and her family (especially to benefit Lisa). Hence Miss Spencer will be asking the judge to come to a decision for Lisa: *"(1) [Subsections (2) to (4) apply[19]]*

---

[19] *Miss Spencer reminds the adoption judge that section 1 ' (2) to (4)' Adoption of Children Act 2002 statutory provisions are*:

"[2] paramount consideration of the court must be child's welfare, throughout her entire life;
(3) The court must at all times bear in mind that, in general, any delay in coming to the decision is likely to prejudice the child's welfare;
[4] The court must have regard to the following matters (among others)—
(a) Child's 'ascertainable wishes' and 'feelings' regarding the decision (considered in the light of child's age and understanding);
(b) child's particular needs;

whenever a court…is coming to a decision relating to the adoption of a child:"

Section 1 (1), Adoption of Children Act 2002 ('ACA 2002')[20]

(c) The likely effect on child (<u>throughout her life</u>) of having ceased to be a member of the original family (Miss x family) and become an adopted person;

(d) child's age, sex, background and any of child's characteristics which the court considers relevant,

(e) <u>any harm</u> which child <u>has suffered</u> or are <u>at risk</u> of <u>suffering</u>,

(f) the <u>relationship</u> which child has <u>with relatives</u> (Miss Spencer and her family), and with any other person.. the court considers the relationship to be relevant, including—

(i) the <u>likelihood</u> of any such <u>relationship continuing and the value</u> to Lisa of its doing so,

(ii) the <u>ability and willingness</u> of any of child's <u>relatives</u> (ie Miss Sencer family) or of any such person, to provide the child with a <u>secure environment</u> in which the child can develop, and otherwise to meet Child's needs,

(iii) the wishes and feelings of any of the <u>child's relatives</u> (or siblings), or of any such person, regarding Child."

[20] The full adoption law in paragraph 3 and footnote 6 (in detail) is never applied in practice after the placement for adoption order has been made. Only 5% of adoptions are ever revoked apparently. It is not remotely possible for these substantive criteria to be applied in reality in a limited time by non lawyers, namely social workers employed by the local government and by Cafcass, also social workers employed by the government. See 'the risk society' and

Miss Spencer informs the judge that "*coming to decision*" applies to her because it is "*the adoption of a child*" (Lisa) by a court (London family court): *s.1 (7)*; It "includes"…"*any proceedings:*" *s.1 (7), such as "an adoption order:" s.1 (7), ACA 2002.*

Miss Jane Spencer representation for opposing the adoption of Lisa: *best interests*[21] *of Lisa, welfare tests: section 1, ACA 2002*

---

the experts, below. There are no lawyers for parents before family court proceedings.

[21] Social workers and Cafcass guardians use '<u>best interest</u>' of the child. A **keyword search** for said terms was used on the *Children Act 1989* ('CA 1989'), *Adoption of Children Act 2002, Children Act 2004 (Cafcass guardian)*. It was located only at section 46 (10 (d)), Children Act 1989: **emergency police power to remove children**. '<u>Welfare of the child</u>,' the term legislators use. It is an important distinction as '*welfare of the child*' implies whole family interests rather than the subjective '<u>child's best interest</u>.'

Lisa's paramount consideration: *Child's welfare for life*

Ms Jane Spencer reminds the adoption judge of his duty to consider the welfare test for Lisa and Miss Spencer '*original family members*' including other relatives such as affected children relatives: *section 1, Adoption of Children Act 2002*.

The *s.1 (7)* decision for the adoption of Lisa as set out above applies to *section 1 (2), ACA 2002*. At s.1 (2); it states: "**…***the paramount consideration…child's welfare throughout Lisa's life*:**" *section 1 (2), Adoption of Children Act 2002*.

Ms Spencer will discuss Lisa's paramount consideration, her daughter's *welfare for life*, and family interests below.

Miss Jane Spencer representation for opposing the adoption of Lisa: Child adoption law: the Threshold

The threshold[22]

Ms Spencer will consider the legal threshold[23] for the adoption judge which is part of his responsibility

---

[22] The threshold law is never considered in revoke, or oppose adoption (final adoption stage). It is always 'change of circumstances:' *section 24, Adoption of Children Act 2002*.

[23] The threshold ('significant harm') in the *Adoption of Children Act 2002* would be defined, according to Khaitan, T. (2014), as an ordinary statute as it affords no checks and balances (also see A V Dicey's Introduction to the UK Constitution') for the state (the local authority; the court) to interrupt Miss Spencer's/ Lisa's child's substantive rights: see Khaitan, T. (2013) at paragraph 592 "'Constitution' as a statutory term" (Sweet & Maxwell (2014); L.Q.R. 2013, 129 (Oct), 589-609. *Each democratic country comprises 'constitutional and ordinary statute' (Khaitan, T. (2013) notwithstanding constitutional case law (ie emanating human rights case law in the UK and USA constitutional case law in the USA). The problem is in absentia of a US style constitution document the*

according to Parliament under section *1 (7) decision (*as set out above*)*. 'Threshold' means the level or standard required. Threshold in the law of children or the law of adoption means the level or high standard required to remove children from families. I next explain the law of threshold.

The law of threshold

To remove Lisa from Ms Spencer the law of threshold must be satisfied as I set out for the adoption judge here. Another word the threshold is sufficient harm. The *Adoption of Children Act 2002* says the harm required for adoption is the same as *Children Act 1989, section 31: section 1 (4) (e)), ACA 2002*. The Children Act 1989 will <u>be considered on that basis. Children Act, section 31</u>[24]

complex answers are found in case law (Av Dicey), and not ordinary family courts below High Court level.
For an understanding of the complex UK Constitution, visit Khaitan, T. website here: https://ukconstitutionallaw.org/2012/01/10/tarun-khaitan-how-to-interpret-constitutional-statutes/

states: "*significant harm which the child suffers or is likely to suffer at the hands of the carer.*" *Section 31 also has inserted "future emotional harm."* Regrettably significant harm is not explained specifically in terms of what significant harm is or how it applies. As the judge's role is to make sense of Parliament law the threshold is interpreted based on related case law ('common law')

Interpreting the threshold at common law:

The threshold based on case law is not clear. However there is a case which supports significant harm to be fair. For example significant harm means any fear of harm by London local authority must be sufficiently serious to justify not being ignored based by its type (*nature*) and extent (*gravity*).[25] Alternatively, the threshold has **not**

---

[24] Harris, L. (2018), pp. 3-4 also discusses the equivalent section 31 threshold of 'significant harm' in England in 'The Law of Children.' (2018) Harris, L., a law graduate has Phd interests, associated with the University of Lancashire.

[25] See Clarke and Morrison on the Children Act at the 'Threshold

been passed just if Ms Spencer has made mistakes or she is <u>simply not perfect</u> ('*commonplace human failure or inadequacy*'): Lord Wilson in <u>Re B</u>.[26]

What is Significant Harm?

I want to say this first, never under any circumstances agree to what family court professionals call the threshold or threshold of significant harm has been met unless you know deep down it has. If you do it will be too late to do

---

Stage' (Part 7, para.40-45, at 'Likely to Suffer'): "*a sense of a real possibility, <u>nature and gravity</u> of the feared harm "in* <u>Re H (Minors)</u> et al." Available from Lexis Nexus materials. This fair approach has been adopted by DWP Upper Tribunal more recently incidentally.

[26] Lord Wilson in <u>Re B</u> at paragraph 27 cites Hedley J in <u>Re L (Care: Threshold Criteria) [2007] 1 FLR 2050</u>, discussing the difference between when the threshold was crossed and circumstantial matters: "<u>*significant harm is fact-specific*</u>; <u>*at least something more than the commonplace human failure or inadequacy*</u>": "<u>*many parents are criminals*</u> or benefit cheats, but <u>those children could not be removed for those reasons.</u>"

anything about it unless you manage to get a solicitor who is fair and does their job properly. Your solicitor will show you a statement that he calls the threshold and final threshold statement. Do not sign it if there are some things you know are not true. No matter how much pressure they put on you regardless if the 6 month public law hearings require extensions. Do not sign unless each one is true. **Even if the threshold has passed it should then go to what is genuinely the child's best interest**. Look, these solicitors are often corrupt and expect you to blindly trust them. The family court appointed psychologists and psychiatrists are also often corrupt. The law for the threshold requires the family court experts' appointments **must be necessary**. The law also is the experts can give an opinion but must stay to their expertise and produce a balance and fair report. The psychologist is not a medical doctor but the psychiatrist is. If it is not necessary tell your solicitor it is not necessary and that you will appeal.

I will provide some brief examples of significant harm and what is not significant harm. Significant harm in my opinion means anything from where children could not generally be removed from families where there is no social worker involvement. The standard is the law of threshold protects families but it only goes so far. A risk means there is a real chance that the child can be harmed whether the child is harm or not at the time. This is a risk of future harm

Broken bones

Broken bones are clearly significant harm where these incidents happen in suspicious circumstances or happen more than once and are not from an accidental injury, are within the law of threshold. This is an obvious example. A broken arm or leg through an isolated incident is not the threshold as many people break arms and legs accidentally and there is no social work involvement.

Some bruises are not significant harm but bruises too often could be or even serious bruising could be.

Parent's Mental Health

Having mental health problems is not significant harm generally. It does not matter if a court appointed psychiatrist or psychologist says parents are a risk. The expert report must be recent for example within the last two years It is not a serious mental health condition unless there is genuine medical evidence for example through registered psychiatrists or psychologists with produced reports to support the mental health conditions. The general practitioner ('GP') will often have them on record. My advice is to not give permission to release medical records if you know the family courts will use it against you. Even if there are medical or mental health conditions they have to be linked to the significant harm. Lawyers call this the causation principle, for example or one thing causes or affects the other.   Unless there are long medical records which go back a long time, say 8 -

10 years or longer I would argue it is not the law of threshold. Mental health problems which genuinely put the child at risk based on evidence could be significant harm. Each parent has a legal responsibility (duty) to take care of the child so if there is serious neglect where a child is not being cared and the child is at risk from suffering that could be significant harm.

It is not significant harm if a parent is not perfect. It is not significant harm if the parent has a random criminal record. The criminal record must be relevant to the family court case: causation as above. If a parent misses dental appointments or school that is not significant harm. If a child has bad teeth or decayed that is not significant harm as families without social work involvement have those types of issues and those children cannot be removed for those reasons. As above being normal or even not being perfect or a great parent does mean the child can be removed: Re B. I next talk about what are never discussed in court, namely human rights.

The UK Government on the threshold

The UK Government also says that the law protects parents from forced adoption. Zahawi, N. (2018) states that Parliament has indicated there are no longer soft thresholds for complex child adoption law at the point Zahawi stated: *"...what happened to 'these mothers and fathers' and 'their children' [ie forced child adoption] could not be repeated today. Society now takes a very different attitude to 'single mother and fathers.'* The *"legislative framework"..."has been transformed beyond recognition.*[27]*"*

---

[27] Nadim Zahawi (2018) at column 1199, 'Forced Adoption in UK,' (12 July 2018) . https://hansard.parliament.uk/commons/2018-07-12/debates/6F6A5DB8-85C8-4AF8-B627-4A8776AD7843/ForcedAdoptionInTheUK

Ms Jane Spencer representation for opposing the adoption of Lisa: Human Rights/ threshold at European level

Human rights: before the threshold

I talked about the law of threshold above. I talk about human rights here associated with the child and Ms Spencer. Ms Spencer for example reminds the adoption judge of what was said about human rights by the former President of the family court Sir James Munby. Munby in Re B –S (Children) adoption case said the starting point for the threshold of significant harm is the human rights of families and children, for instance their <u>engagement of human rights</u>' must happen before the threshold[28] is considered: Munby *at paragraph. 18:* "We start with Article 8...relevant passages from **three key decisions**, *K and T v Finland* (2001) 36 EHRR 255, *R and H v United Kingdom* (2012) 54 EHRR 2, [2011] 2 FLR 1236, and *YC v United Kingdom* (2012) 55 EHRR 967, are set out by the Supreme Court in *re B (A Child) (Care Proceedings: Threshold Criteria)* [2013] UKSC 33, [2013] 1 WLR 1911."[29]

What are Human Rights

---

[28] Jones, T. (2019) stated in other (unpublished) written work stated that the threshold is intended to protect parents against the state and not the right for the state to interrupt parents human rights; Lady Hale (UK Supreme Court judge) also stated the threshold protects parents.

[29] Sir James Munby, former Court of Appeal Judge in Re B-S (Children) [2013] EWCA Civ 1146, at para. 18. discusses Pdf: https://www.judiciary.uk/wp-content/uploads/JCO/Documents/Judgments/b-s-children.pdf

Besides the main law of children, there are also human rights for children and families in adoption and other public law families' matters. Since becoming law in the UK, there have been human rights which you have probably heard of such as the article 8 *right to family life* and article *right to a fair hearing* etc. There are so many articles to list for Lisa's human rights and Ms Spencer's human rights. The right not to receive degrading treatment is the most obvious one next to article 8 and article 6 above. The human rights' articles do not stop there as far as rights go. It is probably not known these human rights mean the articles must be applied something with along the lines o **fair in all the circumstances**.

The human rights for example cannot be interrupted by the social workers or the family courts generally as these go beyond all frontiers (everywhere around you). To interrupt these article rights it requires a '*legitimate aim*' and a '*principle of proportionality.*' Legitimate aim means genuine reasons and proportionality means like for like. The article rights also can only be stopped by *"by law,"* but only where *"….necessary in a democratic society, in the interests of…public safety, for the prevention of disorder or crime"* (ie **qualified right**).

Besides these things the social workers before court or the judge in court for any interference must be *proportionate* and *sufficiently serious*: R (Daly) [2001, HL]. This matches what I said about the threshold above it that must be good reasons to remove children for significant harm.

Also continuing the human rights discussion, '*necessary in a democratic society* ' has been defined by the UK Privy Counsel first [1998] UKPC 30, and afterwards by the Court of Appeal [1999] 1 AC, as requiring: **i)** *justification for any limits on fundamental rights*; **ii)** *rationally connected*; **iii)** *no more than absolutely necessary*: De Freitas. The UK Privy Council is where some of the judges in the UK Supreme Court hear cases outside the UK but considered related to the UK. So this is good law for family courts too.

Child Convention Rights

The children besides the complex although detailed rights above also has Child Convention Rights. The child according to Parliament is the most important (paramount) consideration: *s.1 (2)*, *ACA 2002,* and "..*the most important resource, are entitled to respect for their human rights*, *especially vulnerable and need protection..*" (Joint Select Committee on Child Human Rights, including Child Convention Rights, CHL 117, and HC 1103, (2003)).[30]

---

[30] House of Lords (HL 117) and House of Commons (HC 1103) (2003) cite "..*our children are the most most important resource, are entitled to respect for their human rights*:"
'https://publications.parliament.uk/pa/jt200203/jtselect/jtrights/117/117.pdf

Besides the child's human rights there are also *Child Convention Rights*. The Child Convention is through the obligation that UK has with the United Nations to make sure the child is protected. The main article is ***Article 21***: *right not to be adopted* unless '<u>lawfully' in the child's interest</u> (or the family court has sufficiently justifiable reasons for any 'qualified interest' to interrupt these rights. *Article 3* Child Convention is also the child's 'best interests for all court decisions, and' *Article 7*: *right to know and be cared for by the child's parents.*

Lisa should benefit her own human rights law in terms of the European Convention of Human Rights, the child's European Rights[31] (and her family's, and her Child Convention Rights,[32] in the UK's complex legal or

---

[31] 'Handbook on European law Relating to the Rights of the Child.' For lawyers, judges, family court professional including social workers. Copyright European Union Agency for Fundamental Rights and Council of Europe, 2015 http://fra.europa.eu/en/publication/2015/handbook-european-law-child-rights Pdf English version https://book.coe.int/img/cms/FRA-ECtHR-Handbook-European-law-rights-of-the-child_TK0415510ENN.pdf

[32] The UK Government has an agreement with the Convention of Children Rights: Little Book of Children's Rights and Responsibilities:

constitution situation. It is important for the Family Court ("*the court:*" *s.1 (7), ACA 2002*), to recognise and acknowledge the child's substantive rights as they are clearly <u>necessary in a democracy</u>.

The threshold at Council of Europe³³ level

The European super authorities say that the law of threshold in England is out of touch. About the UK it was said there are "*Developments and concerns in Council of Europe member States³⁴*""

---

https://www.unicef.org/rightsite/files/little_book_rights.pdf

[33] The Council of Europe ('CoE') is super organisation behind the Human Rights Act in all European Countries. CoE took its place by having all government heads in all the European member State sign a (1957) human rights declaration ('to stop any European state including the United Kingdom from having the power of the Nazis ever again).

[34] Rapporteur Mr Valeriu (6 June 2018) at paragraph 41: '4. Developments and concerns in Council of Europe member States' in "Striking a balance between the best interest of the child and the need to keep families together." Committee on Social Affairs, Health and Sustainable Development. Council of Europe Parliament Assembly. http://assembly.coe.int/nw/xml/XRef/Xref-XML2HTML-en.asp?fileid=24770&lang=en

The law for threshold at human rights level according to the European authority for example when quoting *RMS v Spain* for *Article 8: Right to a Family Life* that for the threshold of significant harm it requires a higher standard than normal family court standard. The allegations of harm for example "*must be supported by sufficiently sound and weighty considerations in the interests of the child.*" This is more in line with my opinion on the threshold of significant harm as above.

The law of threshold is out of date by 30 years. According to the Council of Europe, the following was stated about significant harm in the last three decades:

"*in   England,   the   'risk-prediction   model' …councils…assessments…very   inaccurate – 97% of 10,000 parents…as potential abusers did not go on to* *harm their children:***" *Rapporteur Mr Valeriu, Council of Europe draft resolution (2018).*

The child realistically only has rights on paper besides all the law which are supposed to protect Ms Spencer and Lisa. In every situation I have come across with the family courts families and children rights are ignored daily. It is more about just what the family court professionals want. When I think of rights I have remind my self that Men had property rights long before women and children were even considered. Now the UK has not only taken control of education has taken control of family rights. Consider this: if there is control of education everything else is also controlled including conditioning people to what rights are in the first place. Children rights are now recognised in a legal framework. Well usually they are. Nowadays women and children do not have rights in the family court except the right to let their children be stolen.

Miss Jane Spencer representation for opposing the adoption of Lisa: 'Risk Society' – 'the experts' and the State's moral panic, and lies versus real statistics

'Risk society:' and 'the experts'

The council of Europe (see COE resolution for details) as above proves that it is not about the alleged risks[35] of harm that parents[36] pose to their children, at least in 97% of 10,000 parents' cases it is not. On the contrary, it is probably more about how the 'risk society' and how professionals therein define harm (Marsh, I and Keating,

---

[35] Marsh, I. & Keating, M. (2006) cites Beck's 'Risk Society' in that modern society becomes obsessed with risk, and forced care/ adoption is clearly no exception. There are lots of self interests, ie experts, NSPCC ('Making Sense of Society' textbook), 'jobs for the boys?' Sociology, Making Sense of Society text book. 3rd Edition. Pearson Education Limited 2006.

[36] The term section 31, Children Act 1989 uses is 'at the hands of the 'care-giver.'

M. (2006),[37] Goldblatt, D. (2004))[38] and or how 'these self interested experts and professionals package the 'harm' for business purpose (ibid Goldblatt, D. (2004)), or for (corrupt) business purposes. Alternatively, parents in a democracy are not likely to '*go on to harm their children*' (Mr Valeriu (2018)); Op cit Harris, L. (2018); also Duffy, J. et al (2016); [39] as "*core abuse has fallen*" (Dr Levine (2015) below). Core abuse means there is no significant harm to remove the child for adoption.

Statistics, moral panic run state: '*Policing families' and a failed risk model*'

---

[37] Ibid (2006), pp. 537-39, Ch.13: 'Families and Family Living' cites Archard (1993).
[38] Goldblatt, D. (2004), pp.129-31, Chapter 4: 'Changing Knowledge, Changing times' quotes Bell, D. (1973)'s 'The professionals' as 'the dominant social class' in the 'Coming of the Post Industrial Apocalypse.' Knowledge and the social sciences: theory, Method, Practice; Second Edition. Published by Routledge (2000); Open University (2004).
[39] Duffy, J., Caldwell, J., & Collins, M. (2016) discuss the parallel version of the threshold for Northern Ireland. 'Reflections on the Impact of the Children (NI) Order 1995,' Child Care in Practice, 22:4, 327-332, DOI: 10.1080/13575279.2016.1228258: http://www.tandfonline.com/doi/full/10.1080/13575279.2016.1228258 pdf available here:
https://scholar.google.com/scholar_url?url=https://www.tandfonline.com/doi/pdf/10.1080/13575279.2016.1228258&hl=en&sa=T&oi=ucasa&ct=ufr&ei=XG2XXPWSFIWumwHlnaPoAg&scisig=AAGBfm0GuTxv8QH4X3IHirn5WjUSQSqnUw

Misunderstanding the threshold: or abuse of power

There is a clear avoidance of the law of significant harm by the local authorities or social workers do not understand it. By local authorities I mean senior practitioner social workers who make the decision to apply for adoption. The barrister will have advised on the law for adoption. After-all social workers do not do law degrees. However, if barristers do not take law degrees as I said above it is likely they hold a much diluted concept of law and significant harm will be also diluted.

For instance, many local authorities do not fairly apply the statutory threshold for significant harm. Recent studies reveal that social workers blindly follow local authority guidance or government targets owing to recent history where there were relatively few child deaths at the hands of care-givers (op cit Harris, L. (2018),[40] and (op cit

---

[40] Op cit Harris (2018) discusses Baby P, Victoria Climbe, and Scully Hicks cases

Duffy)); it has resulted in a tremendously disproportionate effect to parents' detriment (ibid Duffy). USA research also indicates child protection services may even act on erroneous beliefs (Hamel, J. (2009) et al),[41] third parties do lie after-all (Clemente, P. etc al (2019)),[42] and even social workers lie about child contact with vulnerable children that never actually happened.[43] The problem is that it is a postcode lottery as to whose children will be removed and whose families are supported (APPG, below).

---

[41] Hamel, J., Desmarais, S.L., Nicholls, L.T., Smith, M., and Malley-Morrison, K. (2009), 'Domestic violence and child custody: Are family court professionals' decisions based on erroneous beliefs?' https://www.researchgate.net/publication/236245730 Hamel et al are lawyers and psychologist professionals currently engaged in domestic violence projects.

[42] Clemente, M., Espinosa, P., Padilla, D. (2019) 'Moral disengagement and willingness to behave unethically against ex-partner in a child custody dispute'

[43] Cope, L. (2019). 'Social worker suspended after logging meetings with vulnerable children that did not happen:' https://www.eveningnews24.co.uk/news/health/norfolk-social-worker-county-council-suspended-visits-children-1-5961359?utm_source=Facebook&utm_medium=Social_Icon&utm_campaign=in_article_social_icons&fbclid=IwAR0qd-bbb7OF6Wl9RbGVtltq4EN4hJwZZilmNlmPWMQKbMkxqsQnf24Yqxc

Social workers, in light of these – what are no more than outlier child deaths (or relatively few dangerous parents) – have adopted an exceptionally rigorous approach to reported parental issues, with a polarised result of more social work intervention and thereby more state control; and less parent rights (op cit Duffy); which are effectively 'abuses' by the state: op cit Mr Valeriu (6 June 2018).

The statistics: *Removing children, fear and lies, and damn lies*

The Council of Europe in addition are state 97% of parents will not harm their children (*see above*), the authority's default position for 'policing families'[44] arbitrarily does not support the statistics by 'the initial findings'[45] (Dr Levine, L. (2015) for the removal of

---

[44] Donzelot, J. (1980). 'Policing families,' cited by Cree, V., E. (2000), p.45, at paragraph 'The state, social work and the family,' Post-structuralist and postmodernist perspectives, Chapter 2: Family. 'Sociology for Social Workers and Probation Officers.' The book's publisher: Routledge (2000), New York.

children by the so-called dangerous parents for significant harm. For example: *"Since the children Act 1989 **referrals** have increased by **311%** (from 160,000 per year in 1991/1992 to **657,800** per year in 2013/2014); **Assessments** have increased by **302%** over the same period (from 120,000 to **483,800**); the number of cases of 'core abuse' have **fallen**..."* (Dr Devine. L. (2015).

Local authorities in addition *"focused on child protection concerns, rather than on identifying and responding to a broad range of needs"*[46] (APPG). This is confirmed by government data on children: **631,000** assessed, and **404,731** in Children In Need[47]; **public law applications**

---

[45] Dr Levine, L (2015). Page 9, at paragraph 'Rethinking Child Protection Strategy interim trend analysis results,' Keynote address, Policing Parents, Protecting Children? Rethinking Child Protection Strategy, Initial findings from trend data.' Access here: http://eprints.uwe.ac.uk/25663/1/Keynote%20address%20-%20Policing%20Parents%2C%20Protecting%20Children%20%20%28Rethinking%20Child%20Protection%20Strategy%29.pdf

[46] Local authorities concede there are limited funds and this effect whether a child is removed from parents or not. 'The All Party Parliamentary Group for Children (APPGC) published the findings of their latest Inquiry into children's social care services in England in March 2017.' https://www.ncb.org.uk/resources-publications/resources/no-good-options-report-inquiry-childrens-social-care-england

(2008-2018) since 'Baby P' case: 2008, **20,000**; 2009, 26,000; 2011, 29,500); 2018, nearly 35,000.[48] **89%** of local authorities have section 17 postcode lottery, you only get help if you live in the right postcode[49] (APPG). Officially, less about resources; likely: 26 week limits, red tape and corrupt family court professionals.

Poorer local authorities: post code lottery and trafficking children

There's an obvious link to the strapped for cash UK local governments (councils, local authorities); and economics in that poorer councils will opt for removing children to save money (APPG), in the short term rather than the

---

[47] Page 1 'Characteristics of Children in Need ('CIN') in England 2017-18.' CIN is supposedly voluntary pre public law matter ie before family court involvement. For CIN, how much put upon pressure is another matter: https://assets.publishing.service.gov.uk/government/uploads/system/uploads/attachment_data/file/762527/Characteristics_of_children_in_need_2017-18.pdf

[48] Public law applications have nearly doubled from 2008 – 2018: 20,000 to 35,000: https://assets.publishing.service.gov.uk/government/uploads/system/uploads/attachment_data/file/763391/Guide_to_Family_Court_Statistics.pdf
[49] https://www.ncb.org.uk/storinguptrouble

chaotic state of affairs burdening the country in the longer term. On a quick but slight tangent, there has never been such child trafficking system since World War II United Kingdom, where many children were evacuated to nice parts of the country to be 'safe' from the Nazi bombers' blitz. Children affected by the state in the guise of family courts and or local authority pre court proceedings are far from safe.

I return to the original point. This is the only sensible conclusion given the fact there is unequal treatment as 89% of families are not likely to be helped ('child protection') versus the 11% of local authorities who will ('Children in Need'). Families move to different areas for better schools so may be moving to the 11% of family friendly local authorities' areas is the answer. The problem with that is no one except said 11% of these fairer local authorities or the investigatory committees (APPG) even know where the 11% are located. Hence the section 17 lottery does not just affect where you live for support but also social capital associated with at least the middle class.

Miss Jane Spencer representation for opposing the adoption of Lisa:: *child's relationship with relatives; and Human rights*

I discussed the law of the threshold and human rights and child convention rights above. I talk about here children law in adoption for relationships with family members. The adoption judge also must consider the relationships the child has with family members: "*...child has with relatives....or other person... (i) the likelihood of any such relationship continuing and the value to the child:*" *s.1 (4 (f)), ACA 2002.* This is one of those terrible things about public law in the family courts for adoption. The relatives' rights are completely ignored unless there is a middle class family member who hates the parents.

Miss Spencer also reminds the adoption judge of Lisa's right to communicate her feelings, namely her *"ascertainable wishes and feelings"* in light of her *"age and understanding:" s.1 (4(a), ACA 2002)*.

It would appear that Cafcass, the child's solicitor, the social worker, and the local authority itself did not think about the child substantively in terms of *"having ceased to be a member of the original family and become an adopted person:" section 1 (4 (c)), ACA2002*.

The adopted child is that person who is no longer a member of the original family. The child's rights here are completely ignored in terms of what is right for them. It is a case of just agreeing with the money train unless a middle class family member hates the parents and the child is ignored but placed for a special guardianship. This type of placement almost guarantees that they have control over the parents' rights to contact. The contact then predictably becomes strained because the child now apparently does not want to have contact with her domestic abuse victim mother anymore. What has really happened is the special guardian instructed by the social worker causes an attachment to form where the parents have become alienated from the child.

The law holds value for little Lisa and her single domestic abuse victim mother and Lisa's other family in this democratic country even though there is more drama: "*the key principle…children…looked after within their family… parents playing a full part in their lives. Single mothers and fathers are given the support they need so that they can remain as a family:*" **Nadim Zahawi (2018).**[50]

Miss Spencer informs the judge that the section 1 (7) adoption decision also applies to section *1 (4 (f)), ACA 2002*: "*…child has with relatives….or other person… (i)*

---

[50] ibid Nadim Zahawi (2018) at column 1199

the likelihood of any such relationship continuing and the value to the child.." Once again there is no contact for parents never mind other family members and I have been doing this work for about 3 years. Also see the research below.

Ms Jane Spencer representation for opposing the adoption of Lisa: *Duty to Rehabilitate*

Dual Duty to return Lisa

There were better options for Lisa. The alternative instead of adoption at least without consent for example should have been a duty to rehabilitate accordingly with the local authority's duties under Children law. The duty to rehabilitate that the local authority has towards Ms Spencer means there legal responsibilities owed to her and Lisa, which has two parts (or a dual duty). The first part generally is **placing the child with families when the child has been removed** where it is possible to do so. Secondly, **rehabilitate means to fix the problems for where the child was removed** at the beginning in the first place. The court will be aware that there is also legal guidance from the government in children law named '**Working Together**.' The latest version is the government's 2018 paper. For Ms Spencer situation it meant that the local authority has to cooperate with this government guidance under children law and that would be its employee social workers "working together" with Ms Spencer and her family to keep Lisa in the care of Ms Spencer in the family home.

I now apply the duty to rehabilitate to Ms Spencer's situation. The first part is a legal responsibility to reunite Lisa with her mother; the second, as there were situations involving domestic abuse a legal responsibility to help fix the domestic abuse problem and then return Lisa to her mother. The local authority's duty to rehabilitate should have been under consideration at all times by the local authority. There were for example several points where this dual duty will surface. These duties are at the point Lisa was removed from Ms Spencer voluntary through a section 20 up to the point the judge made a final adoption order. This should have been a priority for Lisa and for her mother as per the Parliament Under-Secretary statement to the relevant person as below.

Duty to Rehabilitate: Foster to Adoption

'rehabilitate the child with their birth family'

The local authority also has the same duty to reunite families in foster care as it does in 'foster to adoption: *"….try to rehabilitate the child with their birth family by supporting the family in overcoming the challenges that led to the child becoming looked-after in the first place. "Fostering for Adoption" does not change this*:" Parliament Under-Secretary for Children and Families (2013) (HL 197 paper)).[51]   Zilch, nada, not in this

---

[51] Parliament Under-Secretary for Children and Families (2013)

lifetime anyway is the child to be returned to the parents. Once adoption has been decided any attempts to put the child back with parents, one of two things happen. The social worker is removed to a new case or the child is said to be still at serious risk. The best line is, 'it has been too long now and the child cannot be returned as they are strangers. Now this line is actually practise and the Norwegian child protection agency used it like it was just normal. It was involved in a human rights case: Grand Chambers in *Strandlobben v Norway* (2019) where it was said by the European judges the duty to rehabilitate is continuous. The UK Government were interveners who disgracefully tried to challenge this part of the case. It is called a ratio decidendi or binding part of the case. I have never heard this case being mentioned in family case law yet at the date of writing.

---

statement to Baroness Butler-Sloss (adoption scrutiny committee), as cited in Appendix 8, "HOUSE OF LORDS, Select Committee on Adoption Legislation, 2nd Report of Session 2012–13; Adoption: Post-Legislative Scrutiny Report:" ('HL 197').

Miss Jane Spencer representation for opposing the adoption of Lisa: _Lisa's ascertainable wishes/ feelings_: *"My name is, Lisa Spencer!"*

Lisa's voice in law

Lisa has a voice in law besides the section 1 (7) right to keep relations with family. For example the decision for the adoption of Lisa applies to *section 1 (4a), ACA 2002*. This is Lisa's "*ascertainable wishes/ and feelings*" which are to be considered by Lisa's "*age and understanding*:" *s.1 (4(a))*. The local authority, social workers, the guardian, especially the child's solicitor likely did not really consider Lisa's interest as what is objectively in Lisa's best interests. Ms Spencer will return to this point below.

As well as Lisa's *ECHR Article 8 Right to a Private Life and Right to a Family life*, her most important right is her own Child Convention Rights, **Article 21**: *right not to be adopted* unless <u>'lawfully' in the child's interest</u> (or the state has sufficiently justifiable reasons for any 'qualified interest' to interrupt these rights. *Article 3* Child Convention is her 'best interests for all court decisions, and' *Article 7*: *right to know and be cared for by her parents.*

Child legal advocacy services: "Sad face; smiley face"

Sad face; smiley face; legal advocacy services

The government view is that young children including Lisa must have their voice heard (Simon Hughes (2015)[52]

---

[52] Simon Hughes cites 'Voice of the Child annual Conferences' by youth justice boards. https://www.gov.uk/government/news/voice-of-the-child-children-to-be-more-clearly-heard-in-decisions-about-their-future?fbclid=IwAR0NBPRWmjWDqxDfmFiGum7VooE7WuUdfktmuHj9HS769ifjWfDcb8gftac
https://www.gov.uk/government/publications/2010-to-2015-government-policy-

instead of other family court professionals doing it, which is likely against their *ascertainable wishes/ feelings* (Davey, S. M Phd, (2015). Very small children can communicate this way: "AM: *"Sad face; smiley face"* and *"Children can have access to...independent legal advice should they really want to challenge what is happening for them*." Chair (Q.30): '*Is there an obligation to tell the children...?*' AM: "*Yes. Children should know about that.*"[53]

The only lawyers the children have is the Cafcass guardian/ social worker who in every case I have come across support what the local authority social workers want. There is therefore no independent advice for children. Social workers do not try and have the child, Lisa or any other children communicate what they want through sad face; smiley face unless it is what the social

family-justice-system/2010-to-2015-government-policy-family-justice-system#appendix-1-the-voice-of-the-child-in-family-justice
[53] Alison Michalska (AM) (2017), President, Association of Directors of Children's Services:
http://data.parliament.uk/writtenevidence/committeeevidence.svc/evidencedocument/education-committee/fostering/oral/71600.html

workers want. The whole system is a joke shop and those association of social worker heads are just very good actors.

Final Good bye contact: 'My Name is Lisa!!'

Lisa has her own identity and knows and loves who she is. At one time it was said of children, "*should be seen and not heard.*"[54] In any event this is 2020 and this writer will amplify Lisa's voice as the family court professionals likely have not. The adopters at the very last contact ('Final goodbye contact') used a different name for Lisa as this is the power the law affords her (new) adoptive parents. Lisa said, *"My Name is Lisa"* (and used her mother's surname) at that final goodbye contact. Lisa was showing her mother, the adopters and

---

[54] Sociologists in the UK witter on about protecting children's rights, their rights to be heard as though children's experiences are a sociological construction (op cit Marsh I. p.372, (2006); apparently many of whom do not have any idea what goes on in family courts. They are likely too middle class to know their arses from their elbow, too busy embracing the modern phenomena of a professional class - albeit milking the proverbial sociology cow, attaining a Phd for something relatively trivial, lecturing ultra left wing matter in universities all over the United Kingdom, and as an 'air of capitalism selling that matter in journals and textbooks all over the world.

social workers that she was not happy with her new identity even before she was forcibly sent to live with middle class strangers forever.

Right to be heard

It is not known if Lisa's solicitor for the Cafcass guardian or the local authority or any of its social workers tried to see whether Lisa's ascertainable wishes and feelings in light of her age and understanding could be communicated to these family court professionals. It is assumed there was no attempt as once the adoption trains are on its tracks there is no stopping them save derailment: Featherstone (2018). After all sensible deductions have been made whatever is left is likely the truth. Lisa's voice has likely been silenced through this forced adoption as her right to be heard in law (*section 1 (4 (a)), CA 1989*, should have been used by the state to engage her human rights and her child convention rights at the point that there was a threat to move Lisa from her domestic abuse victim mother.

Judge remedy: human rights' injunction

Where human rights violations are cited by family court judges, these same say, well this is the point you could have got an injunction for human rights' claims. In other words, a human rights' injunction before it got to court or at the interim hearing stages. It is hard enough trying to get a legal aid lawyer to fight for parents and the child to stay together never mind obtaining an injunction for human rights violations. The only time the lower court judges employ injunctive remedies (so-called 'gagging order' – person is literally gagged)[55] is by default to protect the family court professionals and the judge against public disclosure; although these professionals hide behind the rhetoric, 'protecting the child's identity.'

[55] Katie (2019) is pictured on a protest march against forced adoption holding a banner above her head with the sobering words, 'I Need To Be Able To Tell My Kids I Did Not Stay Silent.' Katie also told Jones, T. (2019) and demonstrates her deviance in the picture, blames the system changing her identity: purple colour hair shaven at the sides with markings. Permission has been granted by Katie to use this photograph from her social media
https://www.facebook.com/photo.php?fbid=1196611337169937&set=t.100003144679554&type=3&theater

If this were not the case why do these gagging orders usually have these types of oppressive terms: "*...the parties shall not discuss or identify the child, or other parties such as the family court professionals: social worker, solicitors, barristers, expert witnesses, social workers, guardian for the child, solicitor for the child.*" The law for injunctive remedies of course has its own tests and standards and this type of clause would in all probability be defeated if there were even a decent lawyer in place. The sad fact, there is a hierarchy of lawyers with commercial barristers at the top and legal aid lawyers occupying near the bottom.

Furthermore, these important laws were likely not applied which is in contrast to what Allison Michalska (see above) said about young children's rights including Lisa's rights in her written evidence to Parliament committee. In any event Lisa was not heard by the family courts or said family court professionals entirely, because the family court did not stop her child adoption; as it did not stop her forced adoption her '*ascertainable wishes and feelings' were ignored*, what some academics view as 'silent violence' as above (op cit Moor). It meant she was forced to live with strangers 'for life,' and not her mummy (Miss Jane Spencer) who loves her unconditionally.[56] Miss Spencer is a not child batterer – not a heroin addict, she does not have a criminal record. She was just a victim[57] of domestic abuse. It is really any wonder that some journalists view child adoption in the United Kingdom as 'corrupt' practice? (Bellone, F. (2013).[58]

---

[56] The 'elephant in the room is that family court professionals get paid whether little Lisa is shipped out to strangers for life or not. Social workers are paid up to £44,000 or much more with experience. Adopters also can get £13,000 (grant) too. The adoption agency also receives £27,000 for to find a match for this blonde hair, blue eye child (commercially attractive).

[57] There is a 'victim blame' culture (Gelles 1997; Dobash 2002)) and or deviancy (Becker H, S. (1963), even in the modern democratic family courts albeit social workers are supposed to understand its consequence for reasons of social justice (Wood, A (2015).

[58] Bellone, F. (2013) is a foreign journalist and broadcaster. Bellone revealed to this writer that she was a child adopter and now alert to what is viewed by forced adoption corruption. See here:
https://www.academia.edu/43375512/Stolen_Children_in_Britain_An_English_Translation_of_the_Original_French_Documentary

Miss Jane Spencer representation for opposing the adoption of Lisa: *the state, social workers, rhetoric, pressure, and commerce*

The state's dirty deeds: 'The social workers'

The 'blame game:' *social workers, stealing babies or a pressure vacuum?*

Social workers: the pressure vacuum

Although there are many social workers, which I have indirectly come across in my work helping parents, not every social worker is bad. It is not however known if they are bad unless the court bundle statements from these social workers are read or there is access to recordings of the same. It is only then that it is possible to gage the social worker's character or lies.

Some quotes from a Community Care article confirm that social workers are employed in toxic environments in terms of pressure, too much paper-work and over-worked (Stevenson, L. 2018). 46 respondents including social worker responses includes, *"Children and their families deserve better, social workers need lower case loads*[59]*"*

Featherstone: *social workers and forced child adoption*

Featherstone et al (2018) investigated social workers involved in adoption and produced a report[60] based on many social workers but much fewer legal professionals' dialogue provided during 'selected' interviews. According to Featherstone the report was made because it was 'time to' (the rhetoric), paraphrasing (see below for a more probable view). Featherstone largely presents

---

[59] Ibid respondent
[60] Featherstone, B. Professor Gupta, A., and Mills, S. (2018) in *"The role of the social worker in adoption – ethics and human rights: An Enquiry"* locate here: https://www.basw.co.uk/adoption-enquiry/docs/The%20Role%20of%20the%20Social%20Worker%20in%20Adoption%20Enquiry.pdf

social workers in a positive light – in contrast to the employing local authorities, or the lawyers, judges, and parents who do not – as the consummate under-appreciated but overworked 'professionals.' This more generous view of social workers somewhat echoes the Community Care above: *"Social workers carrying too heavy a caseload and too little support for managers:"* Featherstone, B. et al (2018), p.13.

As I stated at the beginning social workers are under incredible pressure and there is simply no time to work with public law families, according to Featherstone. *"The pressure on services….financial cuts and rising demand, less time to work with children and families"* and *"manager placed a higher value on ensuring they recorded their work than spending time with families"*(Featherstone, B. (2018)).

It is no longer about the public law families being dangerous either. It is about them being poor and taking children because the local councils will not provide them with the same £450 – 600 that they do when they take children into foster care. For example, *"children living in poverty are more likely to be removed from birth families"*[61]; *"A baby is 'gold dust'* – **what is the level of enquiry/support?** *It can be a 'stitch up'* **(barrister[62]):"** Featherstone (2018), p.31.

Adoption judge: irony and stealing babies *quickly*

Judge say *"adoption is a quick solution*[63]" (Featherstone (2018): *"...in the last 10 years a care plan for adoption is a quick solution and a quicker solution than working with*

---

[61] *"With child poverty increasing, research evidence showing that children living in poverty are more likely to be removed from birth families was raised particularly by academics and organisations in this context*:" Featherstone, p.13.

[62] Other public law professionals comment on the forced adoption controversy: *"A baby is 'gold dust'* – **what is the level of enquiry/support?** *It can be a 'stitch up'* **(barrister):"** Featherstone (2018), p.31.

[63] Featherstone, B. (2018) cites a child adoption judge with decades of experience. It is ironic for an adoption judge to say that as he makes adoption orders. WWWII Nazi judges said they were only following orders too.

this family and *getting them to a right standard of care.* [64]
This involves much more work and effort on the part of
social workers carrying too heavy a caseload and too
little support for managers."

Government Statistics

The Ministry of Justice (MOJ) statistics indicate children
and social workers have on average 17 family/ child case
loads per social worker: 17:1 ratio. In contrast, the
Community Care article, based on a review by social
workers, indicates that social workers have around 25
case loads per family/ child: 25: 1 (Stevenson, L. 2018).[65]
According to Neil McEvoy, in Wales it is a 40:1 ratio.

---

[64] Ironic for an adoption judge who makes adoption orders; Nazi judges said they
followed orders.
[65] Stevenson, L. (2018), 25 quotes from social workers about their current caseload.'
Social workers share their feelings of pressure and high or complex caseloads,
Community Care website, here:
https://www.communitycare.co.uk/2018/04/11/25-quotes-social-workers-current-
caseloads/

Protection racketeering: **local Authority Safeguarding Boards**

Many parents report to this writer that the social workers do not investigate genuine complaints: "*my social worker just ignores me. It's like I am just not there. If she alleges that I have done something wrong it's like I am there again.*"

Even for a serious concern against a foster care for a child in care: '*I reported it to the police but they said, we will come and arrest if you don't stop making these allegations.*' Social services, the police, schools and other authorities work in partnership on a panel so any complaints by a parent whose child is in care is dealt with by a local authority assistant and not the police. At the first stage, it will only go to the police if the – should be but is not in effect – Independent local authority assistant believes there is sufficient evidence. Neil McEnvoy, a Welsh politician, and McKenzie Friend (as above) says the local authorities will only disclose information about offences foster carers have committed if they are forced to such as the media reports a 'bad apple' Social worker. It is therefore like racketeering – a protection racket for said actors. There is an even darker side of forced adoption and foster care if that were even possible.

Foster care abuse cover ups

There is some research showing social services cover up child abuse including sexual abuse by foster carers[66] and adopters. The police and social services covered up child abuse in foster care for 15 years, where there were [and still are today] groomed for sex or drugs done by Asian and white criminal gangs.[67] One 12 year old girl despite

[66] Wonnacott, J. Msc, Mphil, CQSW, AASW (2018). Southampton Safeguarding Children Board Serious Case Review Allegations Against Foster Carers and the Abuse of Children in Foster Care. pdf format available here: http://southamptonlscb.co.uk/wp-content/uploads/2018/09/SCR-Report-Allegations-and-Abuse-in-Foster-Care-1.pdf

[67] Jan. 2020. 'Independent assurance review of the effectiveness of multi-agency responses to child sexual exploitation in Greater Manchester. Part 1:' https://www.greatermanchester-

her grandmother pleading with social services to save her life, according to police operation Augusta, died as a child prostitute addicted to heroin in foster care. This child was allowed to be groomed by an Asian pimp who got her addicted to heroin but she was also allowed to see him as her boyfriend.[68] She is a child in foster care. Something is not quite right here besides the cover-ups. In the world of secrecy even the intelligence agencies in the UK, according to Parliament public record: Hansard, cover up politicians' child sex abuse.[69]

---

ca.gov.uk/media/2569/operation_augusta_january_2020_digital_final.pdf

[68] The local media give about 5 minutes in total air time then this shocking report no longer newsworthy.

[69] The politicians said in 1990 about VIP paedophiles that in the 1970s MI5 knew and covered up young boys in Kincora Homes being sexually abused and ritually abuse in Northern Ireland . This was not reported in the UK except Northern Ireland. See Column 116: https://publications.parliament.uk/pa/cm198990/cmhansrd/1990-07-05/Debate-4.html

What Hansard does not discuss is the boys being ritually abused in posh London homes. "Kincora historic VIP paedophile ring – shock revelations. A Kincora abuse victim from Northern Ireland has told Channel 4 News how he was also abused at London's Elm Guest House and Dolphin Square at the hands of "very powerful people". https://www.channel4.com/news/vip-paedophile-ring-westminster-abuse-elm-guest-dolphin

A man in his 40s showed me on camera over social media his back covered from bottom to top in cigarette burns. He tells he as a young boy in foster he was transported in minibus with other boys his age to a posh expensive London house.

Why should social workers and the police be expected to be different when covering up child abuse of foster carers, adopters, or special guardians?

Private contractors: children treated like cattle

There is of course a commercial angle to all this. Children are being pretty much farmed out to large private accommodation homes on absurdly lucrative contracts. Local authorities, according to McEvoy are paying up to 16,000 a week for difficult to place children in Wales alone. MPs are to investigate why Children are literally missing after 'moving children around care homes' like cattle (Marsh, S. (2019)),[70] the proof in is the

---

This is the secret world people are not supposed to see.

One more thing if these ritual abuse are supposed to be linked to Satanism what was going on then is still happening now.

[70] Marsh, S. (2019). 'Record number of children missing from care in England.' The Guardian.
 https://www.theguardian.com/society/2019/mar/26/record-number-of-children-missing-from-care-in-uk?fbclid=IwAR3xBKhN5bPAcRXRhs1SbprWy1alLfuHzMjBgmjPkNXHRp-FqvQdPUCstaY

pudding. Perhaps the MPs should also investigate how local authorities are making **35,000** public law applications to the court each year just through the Baby P and Climbe fallout, as there is no legal framework in place to stop social workers and local authorities (op cit Harris, L.). The government should also investigate why the papers for an investigation into historic child abuse or sexual abuse by former politicians were lost or omitted. These elites are untouchable as I said above.[71]

Forced Foster care

For a Judas-esque 30 pieces of silver local authorities are putting children in peril by forcing them to runaway, as with irrational young minds there is a high potential for self harm, even suicide attempts, or encountering grooming gangs which may result in UK prostitution or human trafficking in Eastern Europe (op cit Marsh, S.). The reason for this is because so many children are

---

[71] https://www.theguardian.com/uk-news/2020/feb/25/police-and-politicians-turned-blind-eye-to-westminster-child-abuse-claims-report

probably unhappy at being up to 100 miles away from their so-called problem parents even though the law says there must be 'reasonable contact:' *section 34, Children Act 1989.*

Miss Jane Spencer representation for opposing the adoption of Lisa: Before the pendulum swung: - a History of the state, the 'useless eaters,' no rights for children

---

Stealing children[72] **is cheaper; or modern Eugenics 'useless eaters?'**

Look at any forced adoption video online and you will see children screaming as they are forcefully pulled out

---

[72] Richardson, B. A. (2015). 'Interventionism in the Family: Does Adoption Law in England and Wales Advocate the 'Theft' of Children?' 'KENT STUDENT LAW REVIEW Volume 2, 2015. https://journals.kent.ac.uk/index.php/kslr/article/view/229

of mothers arms. Contrast that with this. According to government records, 'when the children heard the Nazi German bombers coming to Hull, "they cried" (Zuckerman Archives, 2017).[73] There are no longer Nazi German bombers or any Nazi German army around but still the children cry in 2020. They cry like little Lisa cried because the grown-ups want to them to go and live with complete strangers forever because of domestic violence not mother battering her little girl. Ms Spencer loves little Lisa more than life itself as do all the other young domestic abuse victim mothers.

In Covid-19 times, we are told to "save lives." Even for the recent campaign "Black Lives Matter." No one says anything about the public law families lives because no one gets to hear the cries of little Lisa or other little children like her when she is pulled away from her

---

[73] 'Zuckerman archives' (2017), Children's letters to schools in Hull: about their eerie and tragic circumstances during World War II. 'Children's essays reveal the effects of Blitz bombing in Hull.' Documentary 4 part series: 'Blitz: the bombs that changed Britain'. Access website
https://unbounddueaarchives.wordpress.com/2017/12/02/childrens-essays-reveal-the-effects-of-blitz-bombing-in-hull/

screaming mother because her mum is just a victim of domestic abuse. The local authorities, it could be argued, are the barometer for draconian times including the current forced care and adoption era. A local authority is one of several hundred government entities at local level ('local government') in the whole United Kingdom. It is the social services or child protection services part of the local authority which are the problem. Local authority practice supported compulsory sterilisation for mums and dads even long after the eugenic (means people are seen as just animals) early 1900s era. Many countries in Europe and in English speaking countries had governments which sponsored or supported eugenics. In a United States of America case, land of the free no less, 'no more than 3 generations of the defective seed' it was said at the time in this USA case precedent. Have times really changed or have the professionals just become more savvy and the laws of secrecy protect its tyranny from being broadcast to the public? I just do not know is the answer. It is at least what Bauman says is a very cruel acquired or now familiar normality as he said of the Nazis in the business of disposing of bodies.

Former Second World War Prime Minister, Winston '...we will fight them on the beaches...,' Churchill ('Oxford Eugenics Panel') said about social workers that they are 'the best of the breed' according to a Canadian social worker's Master's degree thesis. Some pro eugenics in England according to a medical researcher previously discussed killing humans, ie 'death chambers'[74] (Porter, D. 1999). So sterilising mums, dads (ibid Porter) and even their children may not have been so unthinkable to the eugenic conscience. To be fair to Churchill, social workers, what he seen as the best of the breed, currently weed out what he would view as the undesirable 'human stock;' nowadays instead of killing and sterilising families and their children, the children are farmed out to

---

[74] Porter, D. (1999), p.168 at paragraph 'Eugenics in context' in, 10: 'The quality of population and family welfare: human reproduction, eugenics and social policy.' Part 3: The obligations of health in the twentieth century. 'Health, Civilization and the State, a history of public health from ancient to modern times.' Textbook. Published by Routledge (1999)

the middle classes by social workers as social environments help socially engineer the children to be the new generation of middle class. Of course the child must be around a few weeks to age 5 for a successful social engineering transplant. It is though these people (the family courts and family court professionals) are equating parents affected by public law to animals and removing their children away from their wild habitats (said parents homes) and placing them in human zoos.

What is quite sobering is how many social workers nonchalantly refer to a 'liberal state' in reference to substantive parental rights in a democratic country. Social workers simply know the fate of families and children rests in their hands as they have the power, knowledge (Weber; Foucault), and the 3 forms of social capital (Bourdieu) to do just that very thing. Apparently civil people who once call families and children 'human stock' now allegedly have substantive human rights and child Convention Rights in the 'season of democracy.' Not in the family courts!

Forced adoption link to Purchasing NINJA mortgages (high risk)

I said of the adoption judge' above "in the last 10 years…." Let me come back to this. The UK went into a recession in 2008 because bankers were playing pass the parcel with US mortgages (no income no jobs, assets, 'NINJA') which inevitably defaulted predictably.[75] The United Kingdom bankers kept their jobs in England but there was international fallout resulting in prison and other sanctions elsewhere. In any event, it is the poorest and or the below middle social class communities who are disproportionately affected by the UK's lack of financial resources (Featherstone) owing to said recession.

Is it a coincidence that over those 10 years from 2008 – 2018, or 2020 that adoption has become a 'quick option'

---

[75] 'The Financial Crisis Enquiry Report,' p.512

instead of working with families? Furthermore, the likelihood or the only sensible inference to be drawn is that these aforesaid families are clearly targeted (35,000 public law applications) by local authorities as easy prey probably because the public cuts have had different impacts on 89% of the local authorities in the United Kingdom potentially through poor management, or too many overpaid senior managers. I ask again is there still eugenics as the public law families and children do not seem to have the same human value as everybody else. Post adoption contact seems to confirm what I have just said.

Miss Jane Spencer representation for opposing the adoption of Lisa: After-adoption contact: social workers, control, suppression of rights

Adoption contact

Adoption contact: Failed

The family court jokers are supposed to be considering post adoption contact, more smoke and mirrors for the children trade or skin trade, as I call it. McFarlane, now head judge in the family courts, said as much in his annual lecture 'Striking' a Balance[76]' of risk and parent human rights. McFarlane's annual lecture is on post adoption contact; time to revisit.[77] The first case for contact post adoption ('after adoption contact') has predictably been refused by the United Kingdom's highest family court judges [78]in the Court of Appeal.

---

[76] The Bridget Lindley OBE Memorial Lecture 2017, Holding the risk: 'The balance between child protection and the right to family life Lord Justice McFarlane' https://www.judiciary.uk/wp-content/uploads/2017/03/lecture-by-lj-mcfarlane-20160309.pdf

[77] Speech by Lord Justice McFarlane, NAGALRO Annual Conference 2018, Keynote Address, Contact: a point of view   https://www.judiciary.uk/wp-content/uploads/2018/03/speech-by-lj-mcfarlane-nagalro.pdf

[78] I have also produced some work in a different paper on out of touch judges and what I see as regards a segregation (split up) of the social classes, where the upper middle class and upper class are separated from the lower court judges. The

To date there is no child contact after adoption with even child siblings never mind their mums and dads. The parents in forced adoption I help are grateful if the social workers can be arsed to send their yearly letter from their adopted child. The social worker is probably sitting on their fat insecure arses with make-up resembling Ronald McDonald gone wrong, thinking hmm what can I write. "Child is doing well, and loves school, loves their new "forever families, and new brothers and sisters as *"Loves new adopters."* Child hopes '*mum just move on with your life as child is happy.*' The truer unedited version is more like the adopters have abused your child. The adoption placement might end. I will do my best to put her with other middle class adopters, as I have to look good for my senior practitioner employer. I cannot return my commission from the adoption or return my new expensive BMW. I will find other unsuitable adopters

background of the privileged persons creates judges who are entirely out of touch with the social classes below. These judges may as well live in fairy land than understand the problems of too efficient run family court systems.

before I let your child return home to you. I will then fight you with expensive lawyers, QCs to stop you from revoking the adoption placement if you find out the adoption placement has been forced to end."

Birth families ignored by social workers

Here is an example of how hopeless the situation is for parents desperate for contact with their adopted children. *"We felt so powerless in the whole process – even when the judge said there should be contact – it did not happen. SSD [Social Services Department] just wanted adoption – at any cost"* Featherstone (2018), p.23.

Adopters and siblings ignored by social workers

There is not much research in the area of after adoption contact. I did find one. Of 374 adopted children, "*Only 5 adopted children seen birth sibling*;" Of 96 Adopters, many "*support sibling contact…'promises made'… but not routinely happened….. 'repeatedly prompting social workers.'*"[79] This is no surprise as it matches what happens with public law families. Little Lisa was not given the chance to have contact with her domestic abuse victim mother.

Miss Jane Spencer representation for opposing the adoption of Lisa: *Council of Europe – in lieu of a Nazi power; family rights at European level*

---

[79] Meakings, S., Coffey, A., Shelton, K, H. (2017), 'The Influence of Adoption on Sibling Relationships: Experiences and Support Needs of Newly Formed Adoptive Families.' A study was done on 96 adoptive parents out of 374 children adopted in Wales.
https://academic.oup.com/bjsw/article/47/6/1781/4554334#101717534

Featherstone (2018) says the reason for the social work investigation into adoption was just random. This is public relations tactic. Featherstone's apparently random investigation into social workers involvement in child adoption likely coincides with a visit from the Council of Europe representatives to England which later realised a report and an influential instrument (resolution) to be effective on European Member States of course including England in the United Kingdom. There was also a social work investigation in 2015 by the Council of Europe ('COE') because of the European scandal which has been going on at least since 1997. [80]COE is the super organisation behind the Human Rights in all European Countries. COE took its place by having all government Heads of State (at least in all the European Member States) sign a (1957) human rights declaration (' to stop any European state including the United Kingdom from having the power of the Nazis ever again). This was

[80] See my European research here:
https://www.academia.edu/43443705/Council_of_Europe_What_The_UK_Family_C ourt_Professionals_Don_t_Want_You_To_Know._Thomas_Jones_Bsc_LLB._26_June_ 2020

formally known as the European Convention of Human Rights ('ECHR'), and the European Court of Human Rights ('ECrtHR') was set up in Strasbourg, France. World War II Prime Minister aka eugenic was the signatory for the United Kingdom in 1957. I do wonder are rights just a distraction to make us think we are free. What does free even mean and who defines it?

Council of Europe: 'Resolutions'

I provide the following on Mr Valeriu Ghiletchi a member of a family law related committee at European level. Mr Ghiletchi is part of the Parliament Assemble for the Council of Europe. In other words he investigates countries such as the United Kingdom. He then presents his investigation findings to the Council of Europe Committee of Ministers.

In 'Striking a Balance: 'Resolution 2232 (2018), Mr Valeriu Ghiletchi makes it very clear what European law should mean for families vulnerable to the attacks by social workers. Mr Valeriu Ghiletchi (2018) states: *"Article 8... ECrtHR....*__R.M.S. v. Spain__ *that "an interference of a very serious order to split up the family.*[81]*"*

This Council of Europe committee member also goes on to say that to split a family up generally it *"must be supported by sufficiently sound and weighty considerations in the interests of the child."*

Court's Duty: 'preserve personal relations/ rebuild the family'

The family courts know this too but still forcible foster care, child adoptions and special guardianships happen ~~every day. The smoke and mi~~rrors game just continues as

[81] Rapporteur: Mr Valeriu Ghiletchi (27 April 2018), Republic of Moldova, EPP/CD) in 'Striking a balance between the best interest of the child and the need to keep the families together:' Provision version. Committee on Social Affairs, Health and Sustainable Development. Parliament Assembly Council of Europe.
http://assembly.coe.int/nw/xml/XRef/Xref-XML2HTML-en.asp?fileid=24770&lang=en

the former head of the family courts says what the European law should mean. Sir James Munby in <u>Re B-S (Children)</u> *at paragraph 18:* "The judge in <u>Strasbourg court YC v United Kingdom</u> (2012) 55 EHRR 967, para 134 stated *"<u>Family ties</u> may only be severed in <u>**very exceptional circumstances**</u> and ... <u>everything must be done to</u> <u>**preserve personal relations**</u> <u>and, where appropriate, to '**rebuild' the family**</u>. It is <u>**not enough to show that a child could be placed in a more beneficial environment for his upbringing;**</u>[82]* and in Ward and Smeeton (2015))[83]   It is a case of acting or theatre and more a case of do as I say not do as I do. Munby also made forcible foster care, child adoptions and special guardianships before retiring. At least he enjoyed being the headlines every now and again.

---

[82] Sir James Munby, former Court of Appeal Judge <u>in Re B-S (Children)</u> [2013] EWCA Civ 1146, at para. 18. discusses Pdf: https://www.judiciary.uk/wp-content/uploads/JCO/Documents/Judgments/b-s-children.pdf

[83] Ward and Smeeton (2015), social worker academics cite human rights' law: 'The End of Non-Consensual Adoption? Promoting the Wellbeing of Children in Care'. Ward and Smeeton are apparently social worker academics in support of adoptions not being made where there is no parental consent.

Adoption: *must be no other option*

Here is some more drama worthy of an Oscar. I introduce adoption law here first at least you cannot say I do not have a sense of humour. The paramount consideration of the child "*must always consider the whole range of powers; court must not make any order….unless… better for the child than not doing so*:" section 1 (6), ACA2002.

The family court judge does not have to make an adoption order is that section 1 (6) is saying. For instance rather than the judge make an adoption order it must always consider other options which are better for the child. The court in exercising the powers could make no public order at all and return the child: options here would be Children In Need or possibly Child Protection Plan where social workers will supervise the family without court under powers available to social workers under the Children Act. There is also option for care order for parents to look after child at home rather than in foster care. In some countries in Europe, family members take the child where the parents are not able to reasonably parent. There are also special guardianship with family where the parents are still legal parents but security is provided to the special guardians, of sorts they are parents but not legally. COE Ghiletchi for that matter recommends a supervision order which is also available to the family court adoption judge.

Forcible Adoptions: 'Nothing Else will do'

On these section 1 (6) powers, Munby in <u>Re: B-S (Children)</u> at paragraph 22 says "*Orders contemplating non-consensual adoption – care orders with a plan for adoption, placement orders and adoption orders – are "a very extreme thing, a last resort", only to be made where "nothing else will do", where "no other course [is] possible in [the child's] interests*." I explained above what usually happens. It is always a case of the child's age young enough adoption, too old it is then foster care. Special guardian as an alternative is available only if they are middle class and do not get on with the parents. Often now the judge makes more special guardianship orders as too many adoptions make him them look bad. The special guardians are usually middle class strangers. Featherstone (2018) also says the same thing.

Here is some more drama. I am guessing the judges' private schools, is where they learnt the rhetoric. "*orders of the kind which family judges are typically invited to make in public law proceedings are amongst the most drastic that any judge in any jurisdiction is ever empowered to make….:*" Munby in <u>Re J (A child)</u>.[84]

Vigilance: *Unlawful Adoption*

---

[84] More irony as these appeal judges rarely accept appeals. 96% of child adoptions are not voluntary. A case of 'Emperor is not wearing any clothes?'

Apparently judges must be vigilant not about the devastation it causes to the largely non middle class families. No shit Sherlock! *"We must be vigilant to guard against the risks. Such cases, by definition, involve interference, intrusion, by the state, by local authorities and by the court, into family life.* "We strive to avoid miscarriages of justice, but human justice is inevitably fallible.* **The Oldham and Webster cases stand as terrible warning to everyone involved in the family justice system"** Munby (Family court CA President) in <u>Re J (A child)</u> [2013] EWHC 2694, at paras 27-29.

Vigilance: *Miscarriage of justice*:

*"Adoption for life (80 years effect)****," some more drama***

When a family judge makes a placement order or an adoption order in relation to a twenty-year old mother's baby, the mother will have to live with the consequences of that decision for what may be upwards of 60 or even

70 years, and the baby for what may be upwards of 80 or even 90 years:" Munby (Family court CA President) in Re J (A child) [2013] EWHC 2694, at paras 27-29.

Vigilance: 'adoption for life' without consent

"courts must be vigilant and the risk of adoption for life **where the local authority's plan is for** *adoption without consent:* Munby in Re J (A child) [2013].

No injunction for family court professionals

More drama: "*right of the public to know, the need for the public to be confronted with, what is being done in its name. Nowhere is this more necessary than in relation to care and adoption cases:*" Munby in Re J (A child) [2013].

Adoption requires child adoption barristers

These people should be getting paid millions as Hollywood actors as they really do put in a convincing role. I would like to present this year's Oscar to the adoption judge. Here is the drama: "*requires determined lawyers and determined parties* ... *role of specialist family counsel is **vital** in ensuring that justice is done* ...*so...miscarriages of justice are prevented:* Munby in Re J (A child) [2013].

Apparently ancient law of Magna Carta 1215 still applies. How come it only applies to commercial or employment tribunals? Why do not the highest judges in the land ever say anything for the family court circus? Anyway, cue the drama. "Lord Reed in the UK Supreme Court (published 26 July 2017) cites the ancient Magna Carta 1215 right to access justice promptly and fairly, which just as applicable today, 19 November 2018, as in was in the ancient age. "'*In English law, the right of access to the courts.....chapter 40 of the Magna Carta of 1215...remains on the statute book...:"We will sell to no man, we will not deny or defer to any man either Justice or Right*....those words are...a <u>guarantee of access to courts which administer justice promptly and fairly</u>:" Lord Reed (at paragraph 74 (page 22)), in R v Lord Chancellor [2017] UKSC 51. <u>https://www.supremecourt.uk/cases/docs/uksc-2015-0233-judgment.pdf</u>

The Domestic Abuse Victims

Before I conclude I want to just tell you what happens when judges and shockingly even non qualified Magistrates force these adoption orders on the public law families where the mothers are domestic abuse victims. I know many young mums who think about suicide at least every day. When I say young, I mean as young probably as 16 or 17 to approximately to mid twenties to thirties. This is the demographic in adoption. There are other parents in their 30s desperate for contact after adoption. The irony is some mothers have got to keep their other children because they either got good social workers or the judge has to throw the public law cases for foster care and adoption out as it looks bad statistically. I know of one young mother who is so embarrassed by her broken jaw, who thinks all day about self harm as she lies in a bath which eventually runs cold. I know of another who has lost the fight in her to challenge to what will be special guardians. These are also parents of the man who subjected her to domestic abuse now applying for the special guardianship as I here type. There are other adoption problems in the country of Wales in the United Kingdom. The problems in Wales are to do with the local authority covering up the financial benefits of adopters, and in all countries of the United Kingdom problems where mothers have one child living with adopters and another child in foster care and the problems it creates in terms of having a relationship with the families. Little children suffer in the family courts and disabled children suffer the most as the disabled children are the ones the adopters least desire. Wales is a small country and like some parts in all the 4 countries of the UK there are little villages where mums whose children have been taken also live very close to where the foster carers or adopters live. Adopters or foster carers are paid more for children who have problems with trauma for instance from sexual abuse as a child or who experienced other types of abuse. Nearly all the cases I know of are to do with at least some elements of domestic abuse. The UK has a serious problem with domestic abuse and more serious problems of removing children for domestic abuse. Now domestic abuse can be anything from an argument or shouting in front of the child to the father physically assaulting the mother. The courts take children away through "future emotional harm" and this is probably more a "Plan B" by the local authority than an original plan. I have identified a type of "smoke and mirrors" taking place in the family courts where the harm done by the father is ignored by the local authority as it is requires harm against the mother to remove a child also. In that way the domestic abuse or domestic violence committed by the father is hidden with smoke. As for the mirrors, harm is reflected from the domestic abuse father on to the mother to the remove the child. I mean by that, every little thing the mother may have done wrong, shouting at social workers, missed nursery classes or other appointments, or what she has said to the expert appointed by the family court is exaggerated. The more problems children have the more the child is a cash cow for foster carers or adopters. This is a cruel system is my main point. Removing little Lisa and other little children and older children to live with middle class carers or adopters is savage and tyrannous (evil).

Conclusion

This paper is just a glimpse into the secret, corrupt world of 'Forced care and or forced adoption, and special guardianship. This is the secret world which the reader will never get to see unless social services cross your path or you work for the child protection business. This is the real version behind what I go on to identify as a modern holocaust in my coming book, the 'tyranny of us.'

In For Lisa I have presented the law as it needed to be said and done; as the shy family court with its dominant class professionals do not like the limelight. This is the real story behind the media headlines. These are the real problem families not the relatively few dangerous ones (3%), the typically child battering ones the media portrays. This is the real significant harm (public law) in the family courts according to the gospel of the robot middle class family court professionals. The real significant harm is young parents and other families with domestic violence or depression who needs help keeping the house clean or keeping appointments. This paper is for the child I call Lisa and many like her and for the many young domestic abuse mothers whose children are stolen for commercial trade. I have presented this paper from different angles, discussing the real important law, also what should be the law of adoption but in reality is efficiency on crack cocaine.

I appeal to the academics, start writing and using your God-given skills to do something about this tyranny or these families' future generations will be part of another skin trade or child trade in the future.

.